Making Out
in
Spanish

Celia Espelleta

TUTTLE PUBLISHING
Tokyo • Rutland, Vermont • Singapore

Published by Tuttle Publishing, an imprint of Periplus Editions (HK) Ltd., with editorial offices at 364 Innovation Drive, North Clarendon, Vermont 05759 U.S.A. and at 61 Tai Seng Avenue #02-12, Singapore 534167.

Copyright © 2009 Periplus Editions (HK) Ltd

Library of Congress Cataloging-in-Publication Data

Espelleta, Celia.
  Making out in Spanish / Celia Espelleta.—1st ed.
      p. cm.
  ISBN 978-0-8048-4034-7 (pbk.)
1. Spanish language—Conversation and phrase books—English.
2. Spanish language—Textbooks for foreign speakers—English.
3. Spanish language—Self-instruction. I. Title.
  PC4121.E765 2009
  468.2'421--dc22

                                        2008042073

ISBN 978-0-8048-4034-7

Distributed by

North America, Latin America & Europe
Tuttle Publishing
364 Innovation Drive
North Clarendon, VT 05759-9436 U.S.A.
Tel: 1 (802) 773-8930; Fax: 1 (802) 773-6993
info@tuttlepublishing.com
www.tuttlepublishing.com

Asia-Pacific
Berkeley Books Pte. Ltd.
61 Tai Seng Avenue #02-12
Singapore 534167
Tel: (65) 6280-1330; Fax: (65) 6280-6290
inquiries@periplus.com.sg
www.periplus.com

First edition
12 11 10 09 08   10 9 8 7 6 5 4 3 2 1

Printed in Singapore

Contents

Introduction

¡Hola y Bienvenido!   Hi and Welcome!

You plan to travel to a Spanish-speaking country, so you are interested in learning Spanish—or at least in "making out" as you encounter some new places, customs, and people.

Well, for some North Americans Spanish is not a completely unknown language, since they live in a country with the largest number of Latin American immigrants. This is one of the advantages for Spanish learners from the United States: they live in communities where many Latinos have settled. And if you're like many Americans, you may have taken a few Spanish classes in middle and high school. Even if you do not remember everything, you have not forgotten everything either. It is likely that if you've ever learned a little Spanish, some of it will come back to you when you read this book. The situation is a bit different for those in Great Britain, Australia, and other places who may be more unfamiliar with the Spanish language. However, *Making Out in Spanish* includes easy to use phonetic pronunciations for English speakers, so that you can communicate what you need to, no matter where your home is.

It is important to mention that even though all Spanish-speaking countries share the same language root, called Castilian, in every Latin American country Spanish has evolved differently creating a diversity of dialects. The very simple expressions included in this book are usually similar in each country; the main differences among dialects occur in more complex sentences, ones you do not find at the basic level that's taught in this book.

If your trip takes you to the Caribbean Islands, you'll find that Puerto Rico and the Dominican Republic are the places with the closest similarity to Spanish as it's spoken in Spain. Some countries' dialects have different words for common objects, like the word to say "bus," which is **autobús** in Spain, but **guagua** in most Hispanic countries. The same happens with "car," called **coche** in Spain, but **carro** in Latin America. Throughout this book, you'll see the explanation of these differences when they occur.

Even within each Hispanic country, there are some different terms used that other Latinos in other countries do not know. More than the terms used, though, the pronunciation is what differs between Spain and Latin American countries. So do not feel insecure about the variations, because there is a standard Spanish all countries share; if you speak it, you will be able to make yourself understood.

One of the basic phonetic differences is the sound of the **c** and **z** which is pronounced "th" in Spain, but "s" in Latin America. There is also, between Spain and Latin American countries, a different melody to the way people speak Spanish. Likewise, the accent between each Spanish-speaking country is different and even within a country sometimes the accent varies, for instance, in the north and south of Spain. You can make a parallel with the English spoken in the United States and in Great Britain: People can understand each other and have a conversation without misunderstandings, although there are some differences too, especially in the accent.

Regarding the different "versions" of Spanish, you can count on the fact that when they are speaking with a foreigner, Spanish speakers will make an effort to communicate with standard language.

SPANISH BASICS

If you've ever taken a Spanish class, you know already that learning this language has some advantages compared with learning English. For instance, the way words are pronounced in Spanish is not as complicated as in English.

We can start with the fact that in Spanish, we pronounce words the same way we write them. Once you know the Spanish alphabet, you pronounce each letter the same way all the time.

Another advantage when learning Spanish is that some words in English also evolved from ancient Latin; therefore the Spanish and the English words kept a very similar spelling with a different pronunciation. These words are called cognates. (For that reason, *Making Out in Spanish* usually includes the cognate when there are two or more synonyms to choose from, because it will be easier for you to remember.) If a word sounds similar when you hear it or read it in brochures and menus, you can guess it has the same meaning as the English word. However, be careful because there are a few false cognates: words that look similar, but actually have different meanings. Some of those are **librería** which in Spanish does not mean "library," but "bookstore." (Library is **biblioteca**.) **Fútbol** means not American football, but soccer. (You say **fútbol americano** for what the Americans call football.)

But those are the exceptions to a rule; usually you can trust cognates to give you the right meaning.

There are a few cognates that you are likely to read and hear on your trip:

restaurant	**restaurante**
hospital	**hospital**
train	**tren**
basketball	**básquetbol**
	(but **baloncesto** in Spain)

airport	**aeropuerto**
air conditioning	**aire acondicionado**
station	**estación**
telephone	**teléfono**
menu	**menú**
television	**televisión**

You should be aware also if you travel to some regions of Spain, that they have different languages. In Catalonia they speak Catalan, which is also spoken in the Balearic Islands and Valencia. In the Basque region they speak Basque and in Galicia they speak Galician. Those three are completely different languages, not dialects, but in each region most of the population also speaks Spanish, unless you travel to very remote areas in the mountains.

In Latin American countries too they have their indigenous languages, like Mayan in Mexico and Quechua in Guatemala. But most places you visit will have guides and staff who also speak Spanish.

In Spanish, like in other languages, there is an increasing influence or interference of the English language due to media and technology. Some words related to computers are the same as in English, and what's more, there may not even be an original word in Spanish. Sometimes even if there is an original Spanish word, everyone knows and uses the English term instead, as with the terms **e-mail** and **correo electrónico** in Spanish. Keep in mind that many people in Spanish-speaking countries also study English in school.

SPANISH, A ROMANCE LANGUAGE FROM LATIN

The Spanish language appeared in Spain in the Middle Ages, as an evolution of popular Latin. At that time it was called "romance" and mixed characteristics from Latin overall, but also from the other languages spoken in the Peninsula, like Arabic and Hebrew. The predominant trait is the similarity to the basic grammar structure and vocabulary of Latin. There are other languages derived from Latin, all called "romance languages": Portuguese, Italian, French and Romanian.

As a consequence some characteristics of Spanish differ from English, which is an Anglo-Saxon language with different roots. One aspect that makes Spanish more difficult than English is the verbs' conjugations. They are based on the Latin rules for declining verbs, and for that reason there are six different verb forms with ten subject pronouns, for each tense. Another difference is that in Spanish, nouns and adjectives have genders. The article in front of the noun indicates the gender of the noun and adjective as well. Very often the subject pronoun does not appear in a Spanish sentence, especially when it has already been mentioned before. This can take a while for an English speaker to use properly, and to understand what someone is talking about. You can ask someone to repeat what they've said with this question:

"¿Puedes repetir por favor?"

There is also a tendency to speak very fast in Spanish-speaking countries, and sometimes you may need to ask people to speak slowly:

"Habla más despacio."

FORMAL AND INFORMAL CONVERSATIONS
While in English you simply say "you," in Spanish there are two ways to refer to someone, the informal **tú** and the formal **Usted**, many times abbreviated in books as **Ud**. In this aspect there are some differences between Spain and Latin America; people in Latin America use the formal register more often. Also they talk using the **ustedes** plural form of the verb, whereas in Spain they talk using the **vosotros** plural form of the verb.

In Argentina they have another verb form for **usted**, which is **vos** with a slightly different ending in the verb, but the other verb forms are the same. Interestingly, this Latin American country is the one with the most vocabulary differences. This is due to the fact that Argentina has been a melting pot of different ethnic groups who emigrated there from European countries, like Italians, French, Germans and Spaniards. Each of them brought their own culture and also their own language, influencing the predominant official language which is Spanish. But even so, once again it's important to remember that it is the same language with some different words; you will manage all right.

The familiar form **tú** is what you use when you're speaking to someone you know, someone who is your equal (a coworker, for example) and also when the person is not old. On the other hand, the formal **Usted** is more appropriate with someone you do not know yet, an authority figure or someone old. Common sense tells you when one form is more appropriate than the other.

In days past, the use of the formal **Usted** used to be more extended and it is still polite to use it when talking with someone older than you, with your boss at work and with someone you're speaking to for the first time. But nowadays, most teenagers in particular do not follow that rule and they talk in the colloquial **tú** form with everyone. However, it is still more respectful—especially if you're a foreign visitor—to speak formally in situations like those mentioned above.

Another aspect worth mentioning is the different registers that exist in every language. Spanish, just like English, has different vocabulary and expressions according with age and social group. Teenagers for instance develop their own jargon to identify themselves. This book avoids referring to that kind of very specialized language, unless the phrases have now become commonly used among the rest of the population.

DIFFERENT DIALECTS IN EACH COUNTRY

Each Latin American country has their own dialect, which is slightly different compared with the others and with the Spanish spoken in Spain. There is a misconception that in Spain they speak "the proper" Spanish, but the truth is that each dialect is equally correct and acceptable. Languages are alive and evolve constantly, receiving the influence of other languages around them. Every indigenous pre-Columbian language spoken in Latin America provided some new words that were unknown in Spain, and reflected a different reality which did not exist in the European person's motherland. For instance the words **cacique** (chief), **hamaca** (hammock), and **tiburón** (shark), to mention just a few, were adapted from the native indigenous languages of the New Continent, and incorporated into the Spanish language.

The fact is that the Spanish from Spain is the standard language included in textbooks and dictionaries, although some also introduce the most common dialect variants.

It would be daunting to include in *Making Out in Spanish* every term that changes in each country, and it's also not really necessary for a visitor who is spending just a few days there. However, it's interesting to notice these various ways of saying things. There are a few that, even if you do not say, you may hear during your trip.

Standard (Spain)	Other Dialects in Latin American Countries
camarero (waiter) *ka-ma-RE-ro*	**mesero** (Puerto Rico, Mexico, most countries) *me-SE-ro* **mozo** (Argentina, Bolivia, Chile, Peru, a few more) *MO-so*
azafata (flight attendant) *a-tha-FA-ta*	**azafata** (Puerto Rico, Argentina, Bolivia, most countries) *a-sa-FA-ta* **aeromoza** (Colombia, Honduras, Peru, Venezuela) *a-e-ro-MO-sa*
sello (postage stamp) *SE-l-yo*	**estampilla** (Argentina, Mexico, most countries except Puerto Rico which also uses **sello**) *es-tam-PEE-l-ya*
gafas / lentes (eyeglasses) *GA-fas / LEN-tes*	**anteojos** (most Latin American countries) *an-te-O-khos* **espejuelos** (Cuba, Puerto Rico) *es-pe-KHWE-los*
billete / entrada ticket (to a performance, site, or museum; e.g. movie ticket) *bee-L-YE-te / en-TRA-da*	**boleto** (Puerto Rico, Mexico, Peru) *bo-LE-to*

Standard (Spain)	Other Dialects in Latin American Countries
billete / pasaje ticket (transportation ticket; e.g. plane, train) *bee-L-YE-te / pa-SA-khe*	**boleto** (Mexico, Argentina, Chile) *bo-LE-to*
maleta (suitcase) *ma-LE-ta*	**valija** (Argentina, Paraguay, Uruguay) *ba-LEE-kha*
ascensor (elevator) *as-then-SOR*	**elevador** (Puerto Rico) *e-le-ba-DOR*
autobús (bus) *aw-to-BOOS*	**guagua** (Cuba, Puerto Rico, Dominican Republic) *GWA-gwa*
coche (car) *KO-che*	**carro** (Costa Rica, Cuba, Mexico, Puerto Rico, Venezuela) *KA-rro*
plátano / banana (banana) *PLA-ta-no / ba-NA-na*	**guineo** (Puerto Rico, Dominican Republic) *gi-NE-o*
patata (potato) *pa-TA-ta*	**papa** (all Latin American countries) *PA-pa*
bocadillo (sandwich) *bo-ca-DEE-l-yo*	**sándwich** (most Hispanic countries) *SAN-weech*

Standard (Spain)	Other Dialects in Latin American Countries
habitación (room) *a-bee-ta-theeYON*	**cuarto** (Puerto Rico, Dominican Republic, Peru) *KWAR-to*
metro (subway) *ME-tro*	**tren** (Puerto Rico, Peru, Cuba) *tren*
piscina (swimming pool) *pees-THEE-na*	**pileta** (Argentina) *pee-LE-ta*
dinero (money) *dee-NE-ro*	**plata** (Argentina, Chile, Peru) *PLA-ta*
alquiler (rent) *al-kee-LER*	**renta** (Mexico, Dominican Republic, Puerto Rico) *REN-ta*

These are just a few of some of the most common words that differ from the standard Spanish of Spain. Although it's very interesting to notice the differences, you don't have to learn them all; your "standard" Spanish will work in most situations, and people will be happy to try to help you when necessary!

HOW TO FORM QUESTIONS

To ask questions in Spanish, you don't start by saying words like "Do...? Does...? Did...?" as in English. Instead, you change the position of the subject word: you put it *after* the verb. But in Spanish the subject is often not expressed—in which case, the word order is the same as when you make a statement; you just end the sentence with a higher, questioning pitch in your voice. Examples:

English	Informal Tú form	Formal Usted form
You have friends in Spain.	**(Tú) Tienes amigos en España.**	**Ud. tiene amigos en España.**
Do you have friends in Spain?	**¿Tienes (tú) amigos en España?**	**¿Tiene (Ud.) amigos en España?**

Another way to form a question in Spanish is to include the word **¿verdad?** at the end of the sentence. **¿Verdad?** is used in the same way as "isn't it?" or "right?" in English…to let the speaker know that you are fairly certain about something, and are just asking for some reassurance.

For instance:

You have friends in Spain, don't you?	**¿Tienes amigos en España, verdad?**

PRONOUNCING SPANISH

In *Making Out in Spanish*, on the left side of the page you will find the English expression, and on the right side the Spanish translation. Underneath there is a phonetic representation of how the words should be pronounced by an English speaker.

Capital letters indicate the stressed syllable in the word, which should be pronounced with a stronger tone of voice.

The written Spanish language has accent marks, little marks on top of some vowels. The rule is complex, but all you need to know is that these accents indicate the word's stressed syllable, although not every word has a written accent mark on the stressed vowel.

The Spanish alphabet consists of 28 letters, the same letters you already know from the English alphabet plus 2 more: the **ll** and the **ñ**. Next let's learn the pronunciation of these letters, and an explanation of the other sounds that are different between English and Spanish.

LL

The letter **ll** sounds like the English "y" in "yellow," in most regions of Spain and in Latin America. (In the areas of Spain where they pronounce it differently it sounds like "y" but with the tongue between the teeth.) The phonetic representation of this sound is *l-y*; these are some examples:

key   **llave**
                        L-YA-be

to arrive   **llegar**
                        l-ye-GAR

Ñ

The letter **ñ** sounds different than the letter **n**. It's similar to the sound of "ni" in the word "onion" and is the same as the first syllable of the Italian word "gnocchi" (pasta dumplings). The sound of **ñ** or **n** can sometimes change the meaning of the word, so be careful to pronounce these letters correctly! A few examples:

montaña (mountain) **Montana** (the American state)
mon-TA-nya   *mon-TA-na*

año (year)   **ano** (ass)
a-nyo   *a-no*

RR

The other sound that does not exist in English is the **rr**, which sounds like a double "r." It is a bit difficult to make for non-native speakers. Just pronounce it as strongly as you can, rolling the "r" over the next vowel and lingering over the sound of this consonant longer than you would the single "r." Once again, there are some words that change meaning with one or the other of these two sounds, for instance:

caro (expensive)   **carro** (car)
KA-ro   *KA-rro*

H
The letter **h** in Spanish is always silent, no matter its position in the word. There is not even a short, soft sound to it.

hospital   **hospital**
                os-pee-TAL

now   **ahora**
                a-O-ra

J & soft G
The Spanish **j** and sometimes the **g** (when it's followed by the letter **i** or **e**) sound different than in English. The sound is stronger and made in the back of the mouth, like a sound in the throat, not in the teeth. It is like "ch" in the Scottish "loch" or the German "Bach," and also like the sound of "h" in English, but stronger. In this book the phonetic representation is *kh*:

turn   **gira**
                KHEE-ra

manager   **gerente**
                khe-REN-te

June   **Junio**
                KHOO-neeyo

G

The letter **g** sounds like the English "g" in "give," when it is followed by the vowels **a, o,** or **u,** or **i/e** with a **u** in between. Examples:

expense	**gasto**
	<u>G</u>AS-to
guitar	**guitarra**
	gee-TA-rra
war (World War II)	**Guerra**
	<u>G</u>E-rra

C & Z

The sound of the letters **c** and **z** is different in Spain versus Latin America. These letters are pronounced as "th" in Spain, but as "s" in Latin America. (Interestingly, in the South of Spain the sound is also "s"; the first Spaniards to colonize the New World came from that region of Spain, bringing their linguistic influence with them.)

To remind you, throughout this book, first the Latin American "s" pronunciation is included, and second (in parentheses) the Spain sound "th" appears.

Vowels

There are five vowels in Spanish, and they have a total of five sounds. There are no open vowels, nor short and long ones. The vowels sound the same all the time.

So that you can say the vowels easily using the equivalent English sound, the pronunciation guides in this book use the phonetic representation of that English sound. For instance, the Spanish **i** sounds like the English "ee," and the Spanish **u** sounds like the English "oo."

Hi...Nice to Meet You
Hola...Encantado de Conocerle

1

Let's get started with the most common greetings in Spanish. Along with learning what to say, it's also good to know which gestures are appropriate to do, to reinforce your words and also to fit in with local customs. The proper gesture when you are introduced to someone is to shake hands once you know their name and to say "Nice to meet you":

Encantado/a de conocerte.
en-kan-TA-do/a de ko-no-SER-te (ko-no-THER-te)

Remember, the part in parentheses above shows the pronunciation in Spain. Say whichever version fits your destination. Also note that you should say the ending of the first word in the expression as **o**—"**Encantado**"—if you're male, and **a**—"**Encantada**"—if you're female.

To say goodbye sometimes people wave their hand in the air, or when they know the person well they show their affection with a kiss on both cheeks or a hug, which should not be too tight (unless there is a romantic relationship). Do not be surprised to be kissed on both cheeks and also hugged at the same time. In Spanish-speaking countries some people are very emotional and affectionate with farewells, compared with Americans who seem (to the Spanish speakers!) colder in this sense. These affectionate gestures are always appropriate with family and friends, but sometimes also with close acquaintances.

When men hug sometimes they also give friendly pats on the other person's back, but even if firm, it's a soft gesture…not a violent and strong one. Between women it is more common to hug and kiss cheeks, without patting of backs.

Hello! Hi!	**¡Hola!** *O-la!*
	¡Buenos días! *BWE-nos DEE-yas!*
	¡Buenas tardes! *BWE-nas TAR-des!*
	¡Buenas noches! *BWE-nas NO-ches!*

Hola is the most common way of greeting people in Spain. It's used morning, evening, afternoon and night. It is used as the colloquial way to greet someone. It can be used with someone you know and also with someone you're just meeting for the first time. Although **Hola** is used in more informal situations, it also can be used in a formal way. However, there is a more appropriate greeting for formal situations: the expressions **Buenos días** for good morning, **Buenas tardes** for good evening and **Buenas noches** for good night. When you meet someone for the first time these are correct greetings, but you can also use these expressions with people you already know to be more polite. There is no strict rule about it; just keep in mind that **Hola** could be too familiar in some situations, but not incorrect.

Goodbye!	**¡Adiós!**
	a-deeOS!

It has also become trendy to say goodbye in English in some Spanish-speaking countries, due to the influence of the movies. Especially people in the younger generation who have studied English may tell you **Bye** (*BAee*), sounding like the English word.

You may also hear the Italian word **Ciao**, pronounced *Cheeao*, which Americans in the U.S. sometimes say too!

What's your name?	**¿Cómo te llamas?**
	KO-mo te L-YA-mas?

	¿Cómo se llama?
	KO-mo se L-YA-ma?

When you want to be polite and show respect, say the second phrase. That's the **usted** form used with older people and authority figures.

This literally means "How do you call yourself," and in Spanish-speaking countries it is the way one can approach a person whom they do not know but would like to know, and start a conversation. In some situations it implies that you have an interest in perhaps even starting a relationship. For instance at a disco, a pub and at parties, asking this is a common way to get to know someone. In other situations—if you are not sharing a common experience like taking classes, being at the same hotel or in the same tour group—this would not be the first question a person would ask; instead they would exchange other information about their life, before they ask the other person's name.

My name is Josephine.	**Me llamo Josefina.** *me L-YA-mo kho-se-FEE-na*

Nice to meet you, Josephine!	**¡Encantado/a, Josefina! / ¡Mucho gusto!** *en-kan-TA-do/a, kho-se-FEE-na! / MOO-cho GOOS-to!*

These two expressions are the common answers when someone is introduced to another person. Also after asking someone's name and being told, it is polite to say one of these expressions. You can say the word **Encantado/a** in Spanish-speaking countries to reply when shaking hands; say the ending **o** if you are male, or the ending **a** if you are female. The other expression, **Mucho gusto,** "It is (indeed) a pleasure," is a more informal way to respond when you are introduced.

Guess what it is.	**Adivina.** *a-dee-BEE-na*

What did you say?	**¿Qué dices?** *KE DEE-ses? (KE DEE-thes?)*

The second pronunciation is the sound of Spanish spoken in Spain. The first pronunciation is the sound in Hispanic countries. However, in any country they would understand the word said with either of these pronunciations.

Where do you live?	**¿Dónde vives?** *DON-de BEE-bes?*

Dónde (where), **qué** (what), **cómo** (how), **cuándo** (when), **cuánto** (how much), **por qué** (why), **quién** (who): all are important expressions in Spanish, used to introduce a question. For a beginner in Spanish, these words can help you realize that you're being asked a question. With the other kind of interrogative sentences in Spanish—ones without question words—you can only know you are being asked a question by the rising intonation you hear at the end of the sentence.

Where do you come from?	**¿De dónde vienes?** *de DON-de beeYE-nes?*
How old are you?	**¿Cuántos años tienes?** *KWAN-tos a-nyos teeYE-nes?*
Are you a student?	**¿Estudias o trabajas?** *es-TOO-deeyas o tra-BA-khas?*

Very often in Spanish-speaking countries you are asked whether you study or you work—which is the literal meaning of this expression—because these are the most common activities someone does, unless they are unemployed.

Where are you studying?	**¿Dónde estudias?** *DON-de es-TOO-deeyas?*
What's your job?	**¿De qué trabajas?** *de ke tra-BA-khas?*
Do you come here often?	**¿Vienes aquí a menudo?** *beeYE-nes a-kee a me-NOO-do?*
Have I seen you before?	**¿Te he visto antes?** *te e BEEs-to AN-tes?*

The following expressions are used between people who already know each other.

Haven't seen you around for while!

¡Cuánto tiempo sin verte! / ¡Hace mucho que no nos vemos!
KWAN-to teeYEM-po sin BER-te! / A-se (A-the) MOO-cho ke no nos BE-mos!

Cuanto. tiempo sin verte, the most common of these two colloquial expressions, could refer to someone you meet unexpectedly and also to someone you meet at a scheduled appointment, if it is a while since you've seen that person. It means literally "How much time without seeing you…!" You can express the surprise of seeing that person again, so the connotation is more of an exclamation than in the second expression **Hace mucho que no nos vemos**, literally "It is a while that we do not see each other."

The second pronunciation shown for the word **hace** (as "th") indicates the sound in Spain; the first ("s") shows the pronunciation in most Hispanic countries.

How are you?

¿Cómo estás?
KO-mo es-TAS?

How's it going?   **¿Cómo te va?**
                         KO-mo te ba?

Nice to see you again.   **Gusto de verte.**
                         GOOS-to de BER-te
This means literally "What a pleasure to see you," and is the
phrase to use when you run into someone you already
know.

What's up?   **¿Cómo te va? /**
                         ¿Qué hay de nuevo?
                         KO-mo te ba? / KE eye de NWE-bo?
¿Cómo te va? is very common in everyday conversation to
express concern about and interest in the other person's
life. Other translations in English of this expression include
How's it going?, How have you been doing? The second
expression **¿Qué hay de nuevo?** means literally in English
"What's new?" These two expressions can be used in the
same context.

   Either of these is used when you meet someone again
after a while apart, and they're also used to greet someone
you encounter very often in your daily activities at work or
at home.

What's happening?   **¿Qué pasa?**
                         KE PA-sa?

Nothing much.   **No mucho.**
                         no MOO-cho

Nothing special.   **Nada especial.**
                         NA-da es-pe-seeYAL (es-pe-theeYAL)
The pronunciation to use in Spain is shown in parentheses.

Okay, I guess.   **Creo que bien.**
                        KRE-o ke beeYEN

I'm fine.   **Bien.**
                        beeYEN

So-so / Not good,   **Así, así. / Regular. /**
   not bad.   **Ni bien ni mal.**
                        a-SEE, a-SEE / re-goo-LAR /
                        nee beeYEN ni mal

Así, **así** and **Regular** are very common replies when there
are no extremely good or bad events to report in your life,
or when nothing particularly meaningful has happened. But
they can have a negative connotation, if combined with the
appropriate tone of voice.

I wanted to see you /   **Quería verte /**
   I missed you.   **Te echaba de menos.**
                        ke-rEE-ya BER-te /
                        te e-CHA-ba de ME-nos

How have you   **¿Cómo has estado?**
   been doing?   *KO-mo as es-TA-do?*

What have you   **¿Qué has estado haciendo?**
   been doing?   *ke as es-TA-do a-seeYEN-do?*
                        (a-theeYEN-do)

The pronunciation to use in Spain is shown in parentheses.

What's wrong?   **¿Hay algún problema?**
                        EYE al-GOON pro-BLE-ma?

I'm really busy (with work/university)	**Estoy muy ocupado/a (con el trabajo / la universidad).**
	es-TOY mooy o-koo-PA-do/a (kon el tra-BA-kho / la oo-ni-ber-see-DA)

Say **ocupado** if you're male, and **ocupada** if you're female.

I'm not feeling well.	**No me encuentro bien.**
	no me en-KWEN-tro beeYEN

I've got a cold.	**Tengo un resfriado.**
	TEN-go oon res-freeYA-do

I'm a little depressed.	**Estoy algo deprimido.**
	es-TOY AL-go de-pree-MEE-do

I'm tired.	**Estoy cansado/a.**
	es-TOY kan-SA-do/a

Say **cansado** if you're male, and **cansada** if you're female.

I'm sleepy.	**Tengo sueño.**
	TEN-go SWE-nyo

In Spanish the verb used for this expression is "to have" (**haber**), not "to be" (**ser**). In Spanish-speaking countries many physical states or emotions that are expressed with "to be" in English, are expressed with "to have" in Spanish, like **tengo hambre** (I am hungry, lit. "I have hunger") or **tengo sed** (I am thirsty, lit. "I have thirst").

I'm not sleepy.	**No tengo sueño.**
	no TEN-go SWE-nyo

That's a bummer / tough!	**¡Que deprimente!**
	ke de-pri-MEN-te!

That can't be helped / There's nothing you can do about it.	**No hay nada que hacer / No hay solución.** *no eye NA-da ke a-SER (a-THER) / no eye so-loo-seeYON (so-loo-theeYON)*

The pronunciation to use in Spain is shown in parentheses.

That's unfortunate / That's a shame.	**¡Que desgracia! / ¡Que pena!** *ke des-GRA-seeya! / ke PE-na! (ke des-GRA-theeya!)*

The pronunciation to use in Spain is shown in parentheses.

I'll be okay / I'll work it out.	**Estaré bien / Todo irá bien.** *es-ta-RE beeYEN / to-do ee-RA beeYEN*

Cheer up!	**¡Anímate!** *a-NEE-ma-te!*

What's on your mind?	**¿En qué piensas?** *en ke peeYEN-sas?*

Literally, this is "What are you thinking?"

Nothing.	**En nada.** *en NA-da*

When you encounter someone in Spanish-speaking countries using **nada** to answer the question above (of what's on their mind), it does not necessarily mean it's the truth, but more likely that they don't plan to talk about it.

I was just thinking.	**Solo estaba pensando.** *SO-lo es-TA-ba pen-SAN-do*

I was just daydreaming. **Estaba soñando despierto/a.**
es-TA-ba so-NYAN-do
des-peeYER-to/a

Say the word with the **o** ending if you're male, and with the **a** ending if you're female.

Leave me alone. **Déjame tranquilo/a.**
DE-kha-me tran-KEE-lo/a

Say the word with the **o** ending if you're male, and with the **a** ending if you're female.

It's none of your **No te importa.**
  business. no te eem-POR-ta

Is Martina okay? **¿Está bien Martina?**
es-TA beeYEN Martina?

How is Martina doing? **¿Cómo está Martina?**
KO-mo es-TA Martina?

Seen Roberto? **¿Has visto a Roberto?**
as BEES-to a Roberto?

I saw/met Martina. **He visto a Martina.**
e BEES-to a Martina

Let's see each other **¡Nos vemos pronto!**
  soon. nos BE-mos PRON-to!

Goodbye. **¡Adiós¡ ¡Hasta la vista!**
a-deeOS! as-ta la BEES-ta!

Adiós is okay in most situations; **Hasta la vista** means "see you again."

Yes, No, Maybe
Sí, No, Quizás

2

Yes.   **Sí.**
                         see

No.   **No.**
                         no

That's right.   **Exacto / Eso es.**
                         ek-SAK-to / E-so es

These are frequently-used expressions to agree with someone.

I think so.   **Pienso que sí.**
                        peeYEN-so ke SEE

I agree.   **Estoy de acuerdo.**
                        es-TOY de a-KWER-do

So am I / me too.   **Yo también.**
                        yo tam-beeYEN

I see / I got it /   **Entiendo / Comprendo.**
    I understand.   *en-teeYEN-do / kom-PREN-do*

All right, that's okay. **Vale.**
                        BA-le

No problem.   **No hay problema.**
                        no eye pro-BLE-ma

Really?   **¿De verdad?**
                          de ber-DA?

Is that so?   **¿Es verdad?**
                          es ber-DA?

To make sure your Spanish questions are clear, remember, your voice should be rising and higher-pitched at the end of your question.

Yeah, I know.   **Sí, lo sé.**
                          SEE, lo SE

I guess so.   **Creo que sí.**
                          KRE-o ke SEE

It might be true.   **Puede ser verdad.**
                          PWE-de ser ber-DA

Maybe.   **Quizás / Tal vez.**
                          kee-SAS / tal BES
                            (kee-THAS / tal BETH)

These are very similar expressions and can be used interchangeably. The pronunciation to use in Spain is shown in parentheses.

Maybe not.   **Quizás no / Puede que no.**
                          kee-SAS no / PWE-de ke no
                            (kee-THAS no)

The pronunciation to use in Spain is shown in parentheses.

That's not right.   **Esto no está bien.**
                          ES-to no es-TA beeYEN

I wonder.	**Me pregunto.** *me pre-GOON-to*

I don't think so / I doubt it.	**No creo / Lo dudo.** *no KRE-o / lo DOO-do*
I'm not sure.	**No estoy seguro/a.** *no es-TOY se-GOO-ro/a*

Say the word with the **o** ending if you're male, and with the **a** ending if you're female.

There is no way of knowing.	**No hay forma de saberlo.** *no eye FOR-ma de sa-BER-lo*
I can't say for sure.	**No lo puedo asegurar** *no lo PWE-do a-se-goo-RAR*
Because…	**Porque…** *POR-ke…*
Why not?	**¿Por qué no?** *por KE no?*

The Spanish language has only one word to say "why" and "because"; the difference is that you write it with a space and add a stress mark to "**qué**," when asking a question. **Porque** ("because")…**¿por qué?** ("why?").

But…	**Pero…** *PE-ro…*
How come?	**¿Cómo es eso?** *KO-mo es E-so?*
What do you mean?	**¿Qué quieres decir?** *ke keeYE-res de-SEER? (de-THEER)*

The pronunciation to use in Spain is shown in parentheses.

Is something wrong?	**¿Hay algún problema?** *eye al-gOON pro-BLE-ma?*
What's the difference?	**¿Cuál es la diferencia?** *KWAL es la dee-fe-REN-seeya?*
Are you serious?	**¿Lo dices en serio?** *lo DEE-ses en SE-reeyo? (DEE-thes)*

The pronunciation to use in Spain is shown in parentheses.

Are you sure?	**¿Estás seguro/a?** *es-TAS se-GOO-ro/a?*

The pronunciation to use in Spain is shown in parentheses.

You don't mean it? / You're joking?	**¿Hablas en serio? /** **¿Es una broma?** *A-blas en SE-reeyo? /* *es OO-na BRO-ma?*

These are used very commonly to express doubts about something that might seem unbelievable. Many times, the first phrase especially (**¿Hablas en serio?**) is used to express surprise. The second expression is familiar and might be interpreted in the wrong way if the conversation is very serious and formal; it's more appropriate in a less serious talk with friends.

Absolutely.	**Absolutamente.**
	ab-so-LOO-ta-men-te

Definitely.	**Definitivamente.**
	de-fee-nee-TEE-ba-men-te

Of course.	**Por supuesto.**
	por soo-PWES-to

You better believe it!	**¡Puedes creértelo!**
	PWE-des kre-ER-te-lo!

There it is. /   **¡Ahí está! / Aquí lo/la tienes.**
   There you have it.   *EYE es-TA! / a-KEE lo/la teeYE-nes*

You can use these two expressions in the same contexts you'd use them in English. Say one when you present or show something: any kind of object, a place, a person. You can use the expression **Aquí estoy** (Here I am) to introduce your own arrival at an appointment. You can change the verb ending **está** (here he is / she is) to be **están** (here they are) when you want to introduce any group of objects, places or people.

That was good.	**Ha estado muy bien.**
	a es-TA-do mooy beeYEN

Right on / Great! **Perfecto / Estupendo.**
per-FEK-to / es-too-PEN-do

While "great" is used very often in casual English to refer to something that is more than good or that you like very much, Spanish has the words **perfecto** and **estupendo**.

You're kidding me. **Estás bromeando /**
Me tomas el pelo.
es-TAS bro-me-AN-do /
me TO-mas el PE-lo

The second idomatic expression (its literal meaning is "You are cutting my hair") is used very often, most of the time to say you think the other person is joking. Although it can be a friendly comment, with another tone of voice it can also express anger or disbelief.

This is too good to **Esto es demasiado bueno**
be true. **para creerlo.**
ES-to es de-ma-seeYA-do BWE-no
PA-ra kre-ER-lo

That's wrong. **Eso no está bien.**
E-so no es-TA beeYEN

No way / stop joking. **No hagas bromas.**
no A-gas BRO-mas

That's impossible. **Eso es imposible.**
E-so es eem-po-SEE-ble

Forget it! **¡Olvídalo!**
ol-BEE-da-lo!

Bullshit!

Eso es un rollo /
¡Es una estupidez!
E-so es oon RO-l-yo /
es OO-na es-too-pee-DES!
(es-too-pee-DETH)

The first expression is used in colloquial everyday language, referring to something that's too complicated to be believable. It is a very common expression when someone says things almost impossible to believe. The second expression has a similar meaning, however the connotation implies that someone did something stupid.

The pronunciation to use in Spain is shown in parentheses.

Crap / Shit.

¡Mierda!
meeYER-da!

I don't care
(anything's fine).

No me importa (Todo va bien).
no me eem-POR-ta
(TO-do ba beeYEN)

It means nothing
to me.

No significa nada para mí.
no seeg-nee-FEE-ka NA-da PA-ra MEE

I'm not interested.

No me interesa.
no me een-te-RE-sa

These expressions can all be used most of the time, for the same situations. However, **No me importa** can express the idea that you don't mind something, whereas with **No me interesa**, you're expressing that you are definitely not interested.

Now? Later? When?
¿Ahora? ¿Después?
¿Cuándo?

3

Got a second / minute?	**¡Tienes un momento / minuto?** *teeYE-nes oon mo-MEN-to / mee-NOO-to?*
Till when?	**¡Hasta cuándo?** *AS-ta KWAN-do?*
When?	**¡Cuándo?** *KWAN-do?*

About what time?	**¡A qué hora más o menos?** *a ke O-ra mas o ME-nos?*

In Spain and Hispanic countries it is not rare to be late for an appointment, giving a few minutes' window time for an arrival. That's expressed with the term **más o menos** which means literally "more or less." This time frame is still more flexible in Latin America than in Spain. However, this is a habit that varies in each area. Usually in more developed cities and towns the arrival time to an appointment is more rigorous than it is in the countryside or at the beach. This reflects a way of life where "clock" precision is not as important as other aspects of human relationships, like spending time with friends. Keep in mind that in some underdeveloped areas of Latin America they do not know what is to rush constantly, and people like to take their time when they do something.

This does not mean that you cannot find people who like punctuality and expect it from you, especially in big cities and capitals where many citizens have quite stressful lives, just as some do in the United States.

If you are traveling with a tour or you make reservations at someplace, it is advisable to arrive on time of course; the "**más o menos**" time frame refers to other events and relationships you may encounter during your visit.

Is it too early?	**¿Es demasiado pronto?** *es de-ma-seeYA-do PRON-to?*
Is it too late?	**¿Es demasiado tarde?** *es de-ma-seeYA-do TAR-de?*
When is convenient for you?	**¿Cuándo te va bien a tí?** *KWAN-do te ba beeYEN a TEE?*

How about the 18th?	**¿Qué te parece el día 18?**
	KE te pa-RE-se el DEEya
	deeye-seeO-cho?
	(KE te pa-re-the)

Instead of the entire sentence, you can also say just the date introduced by the article: "**El 18**," similar to what's often done in English ("the 18th"). It is a short answer, more familiar, but it is as correct as the other.

The pronunciation to use in Spain is shown in parentheses.

Then when can you	**¿Entonces cuándo puede ser?**
make it?	*en-TON-ses KWAN-do PWE-de ser?*
	(en-TON-thes)

The pronunciation to use in Spain is shown in parentheses.

What time can I	**¿A qué hora puedo pasar?**
come over?	*a ke O-ra PWE-do pa-SAR?*

At what time?	**¿A qué hora?**
	a ke O-ra?

What time do we	**¿A qué hora salimos?**
leave?	*a ke O-ra sa-LEE-mos?*

What time do we	**¿A qué hora llegamos?**
arrive?	*a ke O-ra l-ye-GA-mos?*

The discussion at the beginning of this chapter about a "more or less" approach to time is appropriate to remember here. The time you are expected to appear at an appointment with friends is more flexible than the time for a business or academic appointment. If you are taking summer classes in a Spanish-speaking country, doing an internship or participating in an exchange program, it is required to be punctual at meetings and appointments. But in your personal relationships, be aware that some people may appear a few minutes late without considering this impolite, so you should wait for at least 15 minutes. More than that window of time depends on how well you know the person (or how long you are willing to wait!). If you are really interested in meeting with someone who is late, it's safe to call if you know their phone number; most people have cell phones in large cities and that way you can find out if something unforeseen happened (like delays with public transportation).

| Are you ready? | **¿Estás listo/a?** |
| | es-TAS LEES-to/a? |

Say the word with the **o** ending if you're talking to a male, and with the **a** ending if you're talking to a female.

| When will you do it? | **¿Cuándo lo harás?** |
| | KWAN-do lo a-RAS? |

| How long will it take? | **¿Cuánto tiempo tomará?** |
| | KWAN-to teeYEM-po to-ma-RA? |

| Next time. | **La próxima vez.** |
| | la PROK-see-ma bes (beth) |

The pronunciation to use in Spain is shown in parentheses.

Maybe later. **Quizás más tarde.**
kee-SAS mas TAR-de (kee-THAS)

The pronunciation to use in Spain is shown in parentheses.

Later. **Después / Más tarde.**
des-PWES / mas TAR-de

Soon. **Pronto.**
PRON-to

Not yet. **Todavía no.**
to-da-BEEya no

Not now. **Ahora no.**
a-O-ra no

The last time. **La última vez.**
la OOl-tee-ma bes (beth)

The pronunciation to use in Spain is shown in parentheses.

I don't know when. **No sé cuando.**
no se KWAN-do

I don't know now. **No lo sé ahora.**
no lo se a-O-ra

I don't know yet. **No lo sé todavía.**
no lo se to-da-BEEya

Someday. **Algún día.**
al-GOON DEEya

Not next time. **No la próxima vez.**
no la PROK-see-ma bes (beth)

The pronunciation to use in Spain is shown in parentheses.

Anytime is fine.   **A cualquier hora me va bien.**
a kwal-keeYER O-ra me ba beeYEN

Always.   **Siempre.**
seeYEM-pre

You decide when.   **Tú decides cuándo.**
TOO de-SEE-des KWAN-do
(de-THEE-des)

The pronunciation to use in Spain is shown in parentheses.

That's a bad day for me.   **Ese día no me va bien.**
E-se DEEya no me ba beeYEN

That day is fine.   **Ese día me va bien.**
E-se DEEya me ba beeYEN

Let's begin!   **Vamos a empezar.**
BA-mos a em-PE-sar (em-PE-thar)

The pronunciation to use in Spain is shown in parentheses.

It will take only a minute.   **Sólo llevará un minuto.**
SO-lo l-ye-ba-RA oon mee-NOO-to

Let's continue.   **Vamos a continuar/seguir.**
BA-mos a kon-tee-nwAR/se-GEER

Those two expressions are synonyms and can be used interchangeably. The first one has the advantage of being a cognate, so it might be easier to remember.

Do it later.   **Hazlo más tarde.**
AS-lo mas TAR-de (ATH-lo)

The pronunciation to use in Spain is shown in parentheses.

Let's Go Out!
¡Vamos a Salir!

4

Shall we go and see it?   **¿Vamos a verlo?**
BA-mos a BER-lo?

This question can refer to a person, a performance, a movie or any other event you may be invited to attend. It can also refer to a place, city or village you want to visit.

Did you see it?   **¿Lo has visto?**
lo as BEES-to?

I saw it.   **Lo he visto.**
lo e BEES-to

I didn't see it.   **No lo he visto.**
no lo e BEES-to

Do you want to see...?   **¿Quieres verlo...?**
keeYE-res BER-lo...?

Shall we get a video/ DVD or watch TV instead?	**¿Alquilamos un vídeo/ DVD o vemos la televisión?** *al-kee-LA-mos oon BEE-de-o/ DVD o BE-mos la te-le-bee-seeYON?*

Look.

Mira.
MEE-ra

Look at this!

¡Mira esto!
MEE-ra ES-to!

Look at that!

¡Mira eso!
MEE-ra E-so!

Take a look.

Echa un vistazo.
E-cha oon bees-TA-so
(bees-TA-tho)

The pronunciation to use in Spain is shown in parentheses.

Don't look.

No mires.
no MEE-res

I'll show you.

Te lo enseño.
te lo en-SE-nyo

SHOPPING

Shall we go shopping?   **¿Quieres ir de compras?**
                         keeYE-res eer de KOM-pras?

Let's go shopping   **¿Vamos de compras al centro?**
   downtown.   *BA-mos de KOM-pras al SEN-tro?*
                             (THEN-tro)

The pronunciation to use in Spain is shown in parentheses.

I want to go shopping   **Quiero ir a comprar ropa.**
   for clothes.   *keeYE-ro eer a kom-PRAR RO-pa*

Although the most popular way to purchase clothing is in a boutique or department store, it has become increasingly trendy to go to malls (**galerías**), like in the United States, where you can find all types of stores offering shoes, clothes, gifts, arts and crafts and miscellaneous items.

It is also common to find street fairs or markets where they sell clothes, shoes, food and various other products. If you are a fan of these places you can ask someone, perhaps at the tourism information center, for the day and location; it can be an extraordinary experience to see how lively these markets are. In some cities they are an important tourist attraction, included in guides and brochures, like the market El Rastro in Madrid (Spain).

Shall we go in the center /   **¿Vamos al centro / a la**
   downtown / in the   **plaza?**
   square?   *BA-mos al SEN-tro (THEN-tro) /*
                                  a la PLA-sa? (PLA-tha)

Many cities and towns have squares where people gather to sit on benches or in cafes to have something to drink; it is a very common practice. Many villages on the seashore also have long boulevards with a pedestrian area in the middle with trees, benches and cafes where it's common to find artists playing music, or doing a short performance (dance, mime). These streets are called **ramblas** and in some cities are a very popular and lively place to visit, like the Ramblas in Barcelona (Spain).

The pronunciation to use in Spain is shown in parentheses.

Shall we take a stroll in the center of town?	**¿Damos un paseo por el centro?**
	DA-mos oon pa-SE-o por el SEN-tro? (THEN-tro)

In Spanish-speaking societies, it's a very common social-interaction event to go for a walk to the center, especially to the boulevards mentioned above where people of every age and status like to spend their time after work or during the weekend. It is typical to walk up and down these streets, sit on benches for a while or in outdoor cafes, chatting with friends and watching people passing by. Some local artists sell their goods—pictures, paintings, t-shirts, etc.—on the ground or at small stands.

The pronunciation to use in Spain is shown in parentheses.

Shall we go for a coffee / for an ice cream / to a pastry shop?	**¿Vamos a tomar un café / a comer un helado / a la pastelería?**
	BA-mos a to-MAR oon ka-FE / a ko-MER oon e-LA-do / a la pas-te-le-REEYA?

Many times in Spanish-speaking countries people offer this type of invitation, meaning that they want to hang out with someone while having something to drink or eat. Even though this could be considered a date, it is not as formal as going out for dinner, and it has a friendly connotation.

Shall we go for a drink?   **¿Vamos a beber algo?**
                            BA-mos a be-BER AL-go?

This is the common way to invite someone to go out to have a drink, which can refer to the time of day for having an appetizer (**aperitivo**), a very extended practice of eating something light like **tapas** before lunch in a café, especially on Sunday morning or afternoon. If you are not aware of this type of snack you should definitely ask for it; it is very common and popular in Spain. In some regions they have a great diversity of **tapas**, for instance in Andalucia and the Basque region due to their rich fishing industry.

In the evening and night, "going out for a drink" can mean to have a beer, wine or another type of refreshment, including alcoholic beverages. In this case the invitation can have a completely different intention and it is safe to be prepared, since it implies that the person is interested in deepening the relationship or friendship. It is convenient if you want to avoid future misunderstandings not to accept this type of invitation if you are not really interested in the person.

Shall we go get something?   **¿Vamos a tomar algo?**
                              BA-mos a to-MAR AL-go?

This expression is very similar to the previous one and can be used in the same situations.

I wonder where we should go.

Me pregunto adónde deberíamos ir.
me pre-GOON-to a-DON-de de-be-reeYA-mos eer

I know a good place.

Conozco un buen sitio.
ko-NOS-ko oon bwen SEE-teeyo

Shall we go clubbing this Friday/ Saturday?

¿Quieres ir a la discoteca / a bailar este viernes/ sábado?
keeYE-res eer a la dees-ko-TE-ka / a baee-LAR ES-te beeYER-nes/ SA-ba-do?

Let's go to your favorite club.

Vamos a tu bar/pub favorito.
BA-mos a too bar/pub fa-bo-REE-to

Spanish does have the word "club," but since that can have different meanings, it's best to say **bar** in this context instead. A **club** can refer to a social club, sports club or nightclub. A nightclub is really a very common place to go with friends, but most of the time it's termed a **pub**; you can listen to good music and sometimes they also offer live music. These words show one of the many ways English has influenced the Spanish language, and even the social life of Spanish-speaking countries.

Talk to Me!
¡Háblame!

5

Talk to me.

Dime / Háblame.
DEE-me / A-bla-me

These two expressions are both common, but the first one is the more familiar and less serious of them. **Dime** can be said when another person starts to talk, to show your interest and make him/her know that you want to listen. **Háblame** might be used a bit more earnestly, for example, when one thinks the other person needs to talk about private issues, but is not doing so yet. It's like asking the other person to share, to open up with you.

Listen.

Escucha.
es-KOO-cha

Listen to me.

Escúchame
es-KOO-cha-me

Don't ask me that.

No me preguntes eso.
no me pre-GOON-tes E-so

If someone asks something you do not want to answer for any reason, this could be the most polite expression to use to keep your thoughts and your opinions to yourself. It could imply that you cannot talk about it because someone told you not to. It can also mean that this is a private issue you simply do not want to discuss. If the other person is tactful he/she won't insist any longer and will accept your reply.

Did you hear me? / him/her?	**¿Me has oído? /** **¿Lo/la has oído?**
	me as o-EE-do? / lo/la as o-EE-do?

To say "him" you would ask with **lo**, and to say "her" you would ask with **la**.

I couldn't hear.	**No he podido oirlo.**
	no e po-DEE-do o-EER-lo

I don't want to hear.	**No quiero escucharlo/oirlo.**
	no keeYE-ro es-koo-CHAR-lo/o-EER-lo

Speak up.	**Habla más alto.**
	A-bla mas AL-to

Speak more slowly.	**Habla más despacio.**
	A-bla mas des-PA-seeyo
	(des-PA-theeyo)

The pronunciation to use in Spain is shown in parentheses.

Say it again.	**¿Puedes repetirlo?**
	PWE-des re-pe-TEER-lo?

Let's talk in Spanish.	**Hablemos en español.**
	a-BLE-mos en es-pa-NYOL

Your Spanish is really good.	**Hablas muy bien español.**
	A-blas mooy beeYEN es-pa-NYOL

Let's talk in English.	**Hablemos en inglés.**
	a-BLE-mos en een-GLES

It is very normal to find people who know some English in Spanish-speaking countries. Especially for a tourist visiting the main attractions and cities, it's common to find staff in hotels and airports who speak at least the very basic English expressions useful for communicating with foreigners. Keep in mind that in Spain children start to learn English in elementary school, although the level they achieve in public schools is not usually very good. In Latin America there are countries like Puerto Rico where most of the population is bilingual. Other countries not closely associated with the U.S., like the Dominican Republic, also have an increasing number of people who study English, but that happens mostly in more educated segments of society and especially within the tourist industry. It would not be common to find elderly people who know English, whether you're in main cities or remote villages.

You are good at English.	**Hablas bien en inglés.** *A-blas beeYEN en een-GLES*
Yes, you really are good.	**Sí, eres realmente bueno.** *SEE, E-res re-al-MEN-te BWE-no*
Where did you learn English?	**¿Dónde has aprendido el inglés?** *DON-de as a-pren-DEE-do el een-GLES?*
How long have you been learning English?	**¿Cuánto tiempo hace que estudias inglés?** *KWAN-to teeYEM-po A-se ke es-TOO-deeyas een-GLES?* *(A-the)*

The pronunciation to use in Spain is shown in parentheses.

Say something.	**Di algo.** *dee AL-go*

Have you studied English in America or in the U.K.?	**¿Has estudiado inglés en América o en el Reino Unido?** *as es-too-deeYA-do een-GLES en a-ME-ri-ka o en el RE-ee-no OO-NEE-do?*
What are you talking about?	**¿De qué estás hablando?** *de ke es-TAS a-BLAN-do?*
Let's keep talking about it.	**Seguimos hablando de ello.** *se-GEE-mos a-BLAN-do de e-l-yo*
Let's talk about it later.	**Hablamos de eso más tarde.** *a-BLA-mos de e-so mas TAR-de*
I don't want to talk.	**No quiero hablar.** *no keeYE-ro a-BLAR*
I don't want to talk about it.	**No quiero hablar de eso.** *no keeYE-ro a-BLAR de e-so*
By the way...	**A propósito...** *a pro-PO-see-to...*
Just to change the subject...	**Cambiando de tema...** *kam-beeYAN-do de TE-ma...*

When someone does not want to talk about a topic any more, this is the appropriate expression to let the others know that you're finished. It could be because you've already discussed it for too long and there's no more to say, or because the conversation is making any of the speakers uncomfortable. Sometimes it could just mean that the person suddenly remembers something else he doesn't want to forget to tell.

But also the change of subject could be due to the fact that the conversation is becoming tense and argumentative, so it is a way to avoid a quarrel. If this is the case, the next expression is a suitable one.

Please, don't get upset... **Por favor, no te enfades...**
por fa-BOR, no te en-FA-des...

Nice weather... **Hace buen tiempo...**
A-se bwen teeYEM-po... (A-the)

The pronunciation to use in Spain is shown in parentheses, here and for several of the next phrases.

When are you going **¿Cuándo te vas de vacaciones?**
on vacation? *KWAN-do te bas de ba-ka-seeYO-
nes? (ba-ka-theeYO-nes)*

It is getting late... / **Se hace tarde... /**
I need to go. **Me tengo que ir.**
*se A-se TAR-de... /
me TEN-go ke eer (A-the)*

Some of the previous expressions are attemps to smooth the tension with small talk. However this one could be an abrupt way to say goodbye if the conversation is getting really uncomfortable. The next expressions can be useful to let the other person know you are getting angry or at least uneasy.

Do not make excuses. **No me vengas con excusas.**
no me BEN-gas kon eks-KOO-sas

That's not a good **Esa no es una buena excusa.**
excuse. *E-sa no es OO-na BWE-na
eks-KOO-sa*

Stop complaining! **¡Deja de quejarte!**
DE-kha de ke-KHAR-te!

Do you know what **¿Sabes lo que estás diciendo?**
you are saying? *SA-bes lo ke es-TAS dee-seeYEN-do?*
(dee-theeYEN-do)

With a hostile tone of voice, this expression can suggest
that the other person has said something out of line.

The pronunciation to use in Spain is shown in parentheses.

You said that, **¿Lo has dicho tú, verdad?**
didn't you? *lo as DEE-cho too, ber-DA?*

The English tag questions, like "didn't you," are expressed in
Spanish with the word **verdad** at the end of the phrase. It
is very common to end question sentences in Spanish with
this word. A more complicated expression with the same
function is **¿a qué sí?**, also said at the end of the question.

I didn't say anything. **No he dicho nada.**
no e DEE-cho NA-da

You'd better not say things like that.	**Harías mejor en no decir cosas como esas.**
	a-REEYAS me-KHOR en no de-SEER KO-sas KO-mo E-sas (de-THEER)

This could also be a very hostile and provocative phrase, if said with a certain tone of voice. However, with a pleasant tone of voice it could be friendly advice to someone you care about, to help them stay out of trouble.

The pronunciation to use in Spain is shown in parentheses.

Don't say things like that.	**No digas cosas como esas.**
	no DEE-gas KO-sas KO-mo E-sas

Don't talk so loudly.	**No hables tan alto.**
	no A-bles tan AL-to

There is some tendency among uneducated people in Spanish-speaking countries to speak loudly and sometimes even scream at each other when arguing about a subject. But if someone has the appropriate arguments to support his or her ideas about a topic, usually the person is also able to control the passion that could trigger the heat of a quarrel. However, even some highly educated people turn up the volume in their conversations when the discussion involves very controversial subjects. Do not be surprised if you hear Spanish speakers in this situation talking at the same time without listening to one another!

Coming and Going
Ir y Venir

6

Come here.
Ven aquí.
ben a-KEE

Come over.
Ven por aquí.
ben por a-KEE

Come later.
Ven después / más tarde.
ben des-PWES / mas TAR-de

In this expression you can use **después** and **más tarde** interchangeably.

Can you come?
¿Puedes venir?
PWE-des be-NEER?

Won't you come with me/us?
¿No quieres venir conmigo / con nosotros?
no keeYE-res be-NEER kon-MEE-go / kon no-SO-tros?

She/he is coming here.
Ella/Él viene aquí.
E-l-ya/El beeYE-ne a-KEE

I'm coming, wait a second.
Ya voy, espera un segundo.
ya BOY, es-PE-ra oon se-GOON-do

I can go.
Puedo ir.
PWE-do eer

I think I can go.	**Creo que puedo ir.** *KRE-o ke PWE-do eer*
I can't go.	**No puedo ir.** *no PWE-do eer*
I want to go.	**Quiero ir.** *keeYE-ro eer*

I want to go to
  Madrid / Santo
  Domingo / Lima.
	**Quiero ir a Madrid /
	  Santo Domingo / Lima.**
	*keeYE-ro eer a ma-DREE /
	  SAN-to do-MEEN-go / LEE-ma*

I really want to go.	**Realmente quiero ir.** *re-al-MEN-te keeYE-ro eer*
I don't want to go.	**No quiero ir.** *no keeYE-ro eer*
You went, didn't you?	**¿Tú fuiste, verdad?** *too fwEES-te, ber-DA?*
I went.	**Yo fui.** *yo fwEE*

By the way, this is also how you say "I was" (since the verb
"to go" has the same form as the verb "to be," just in this
tense). Whenever you hear this phrase, the context is going
to let you know the meaning.

I didn't go.	**No fui.** *no fwEE*

Don't go.   **No vayas.**
                   no BA-yas

Don't go yet.   **No vayas todavía/aún.**
                   no BA-yas to-da-BEEya / aOON

You can use the words **todavía** and **aún** interchangeably in this expression.

I have to go now.   **Tengo que irme ahora.**
                   TEN-go ke EER-me a-O-ra

The letter **h** in Spanish is silent, whether it is at the beginning of the word or in the middle.

May I go?   **¿Puedo irme?**
                   PWE-do EER-me?

Shall we go?   **¿Nos vamos?**
                   nos BA-mos?

Let's go.   **Vámonos.**
                   BA-mo-nos

Let's get out of here /   **Vámonos de aquí.**
    leave.   *BA-mo-nos de a-KEE*

I'm leaving soon.   **Me voy pronto.**
                   me boy PRON-to

She/he has left here.   **Ella/Él se ha ido de aquí.**
                   E-l-ya/El se a EE-do de a-KEE

She/he has gone home.   **Ella/Él se ha ido a casa.**
                   E-l-ya/El se a EE-do a KA-sa

Where are you going?	**¿Adónde vas?**
	a-DON-de bas?

Please go first. / After you.	**Por favor, tú/Usted primero. /** **Después de tí.**
	por fa-BOR, too/oos-TE pree-ME-ro / *des-PWES de tee*

The difference between **tú** and **Usted** is that the first is informal and the second is formal. You can find a more extensive explanation of these words in the Introduction.

Thanks for letting me go first.	**Gracias por dejarme ir** **primero.**
	GRA-seeyas por de-KHAR-me eer *pree-ME-ro (GRA-theeyas)*

The pronunciation to use in Spain is shown in parentheses.

Take your time / Go slowly.	**Tomate tu tiempo /** **Ves despacio.**
	TO-ma-te too teeYEM-po / *bes des-PA-seeyo (des-PA-theeyo)*

The pronunciation to use in Spain is shown in parentheses.

I'm lost.	**Estoy perdido/a.**
	es-TOY per-DEE-do/a

Say the word with the **o** ending if you're male, and with the **a** ending if you're female.

Please tell me the way.	**Por favor, dígame cómo llegar.**
	por fa-BOR, DEE-ga-me KO-mo *l-ye-GAR*

You can ask this question after stating the place where you are going. Or you can say it at the beginning, and then name the place or street you are asking directions to.

Could you write it down?	**¿Puede escribirlo por favor?** *PWE-de es-kree-BEER-lo por fa-BOR?*

When asking directions in Spanish it is polite to say **Por favor** (please), either at the beginning or at the end.

Please tell me the train station name.	**Por favor, dígame el nombre de la estación de tren.** *por fa-BOR, DEE-ga-me el NOM-bre de la es-ta-seeYON de tren (es-ta-theeYON)*

When addressing someone you do not know it is more appropriate to talk in the formal (**Usted**) register, as in this expression ("dígame"). However if you ask someone who is young it would not be incorrect to use the informal **tú** form "dime." To be safe and very polite you may want to use the formal version with everyone, until you know them.

The pronunciation to use in Spain is shown in parentheses.

Which train/bus should I take?	**¿Qué tren/autobús debo tomar/coger?** *ke tren/aw-to-BOOS DE-bo to-MAR/ko-KHER?*

The word **autobús** is the standard translation for "bus." However, many Hispanic countries have their dialects with different terms, and "bus" is called **guagua** in many Caribbean and Latin American countries.

Get off at [station]... / [bus stop]...	**Bájate en la estación ... / parada de autobús (guagua) ...** *BA-kha-te en la es-ta-seeYON ... / pa-RA-da de aw-to-BOOS (GWA-gwa) ...*

For the next phrases too, remember that in most Hispanic countries the bus is called **guagua**, so you'd say that instead; however, the word **autobús** is the standard term in Spanish.

In Spain, pronounce the word **estación** like this: *es-ta-theeYON*.

How will I know when to get off?	**¿Cómo sabré dónde bajarme?** *KO-mo sa-BRE DON-de ba-KHAR-me?*
You'll hear the station name announced on the train.	**Oirás el nombre de la estación anunciada en el tren.** *oee-RAS el NOM-bre de la es-ta-seeYON a-noon-seeYA-da en el tren (es-ta-theeYON) … (a-noon-theeYA-da)*
You'd better ask the bus driver.	**Es mejor preguntar al conductor.** *es me-KHOR pre-GOON-tar al kon-dook-TOR*
How much does the ticket/ride cost?	**¿Cuánto cuesta el billete (boleto)?** *KWAN-to kwES-ta el bee-l-YE-te (bo-LE-to)?*

In standard language (Spain), **billete** refers to "ticket" for transportation. In most Hispanic dialects, the word **boleto** is used instead, and it is also the word for a ticket to a performance, like a concert, movie, theater, or a sports event. In Spain, the term for that meaning is **entrada**.

Eat, Drink, Be Merry
Come, Bebe, Disfruta la Vida

7

In Spanish-speaking countries there is a hedonistic idea of how to enjoy life. It's based on a Mediterranean or a pre-Columbian culture that historically placed emphasis on farmers' festivities after their crops were harvested. The ritual has evolved through the centuries, but luckily for visitors, this custom still places food at the center of any social gathering and celebration, whether in the countryside or in the cities.

Many of the most celebrated festivities have religious roots; in all of them having a meal is the most important ingredient of the event, with music and dance. The Spaniard-style habits can also be found in Hispanic countries, where the culture of the colonizers has been mixed with their pre-Columbian roots.

There are several aspects to take into account as far as meals in Spanish-speaking countries go. One difference from Anglo-Saxon culture is the timing; each meal (except for breakfast) usually is eaten later than in the United States. However, if your trip is to Puerto Rico, keep in mind that it's a Hispanic country with customs more similar to North America, since it is also a territory of the United States.

It is uncommon to eat lunch at 11 A.M. or noon, which is still "breakfast time" in Spanish-speaking countries. The usual lunch hour range goes from 1:00 to 3:00 P.M., and in some restaurants at the beach you can find lunch served at four. Dinner can start at eight or nine, but it is certainly not usual to start eating at six or seven. At that time it is common instead to have a type of snack called **merienda** which can be similar to breakfast (coffee and bread or pastry); in addition some coffee shops in Spain serve hot chocolate, very thick, with any pastry. If your travel takes you to Catalonia and the Balearic Islands, you can taste the **ensiamada**, a Mallorcan pastry.

The other relevant difference is the relative importance of each of the meals of the day, and therefore the quantity of food normally consumed. Breakfast is not as abundant as in Anglo-Saxon cultures: usually along with coffee one has a pastry or toast, not eggs and bacon. The Spanish tradition places lunch as the most important meal of the day, rather than breakfast or dinner. Meal habits are changing with the present times, adapting to the demands of the working world and becoming more similar to the American lifestyle. In large cities where most women work and are forced to eat outside the home, the American customs are increasingly dominant.

I'm hungry.	**Tengo hambre.**
	TEN-go AM-bre

The **h** is always silent in Spanish, no matter its position.

I'd like to eat something.	**Me gustaría comer algo.**
	me goos-ta-REEya ko-MER AL-go
I haven't eaten yet.	**No he comido aún.**
	no e ko-MEE-do aOON
Do you want to eat?	**¿Quieres comer algo?**
	keeYE-res ko-MER AL-go?
I don't want to eat now.	**No quiero comer ahora.**
	no keeYE-ro ko-MER a-O-ra

Did you eat lunch?   **¿Has comido? ¿Has cenado?**
  Dinner?   *as ko-MEE-do? as se-NA-do?*
                       (the-NA-do)

The pronunciation to use in Spain is shown in parentheses.

What would you like? **¿Qué te apetece?**
                      ke te a-pe-TE-se? (a-pe-TE-the)

The pronunciation to use in Spain is shown in parentheses.

I'm thirsty.   **Tengo sed.**
                      TEN-go sed

The expressions of feelings and states in English use the verb "to be": "I am thirsty." However, in Spanish these expressions use the verb **tener**, literally "to have": "I have thirst."

I'd like some wine/   **Quiero vino/cerveza.**
  a beer.   *keeYE-ro BEE-no/ser-BE-sa*
                      (ther-BE-tha)

The pronunciation to use in Spain is shown in parentheses.

I'd like a soft drink/   **Quiero un refresco/**
  cola/coffee/tea.   **coca-cola/café/té.**
                         keeYE-ro oon re-FRES-ko /
                         ko-ka-ko-la / ka-FE / te

In Spanish-speaking countries it is more popular to have coffee than tea, but you can also find a minority of the population who prefers the English habit of having tea instead.

There are also local beverages to try, for example the herbal drink called **mate** that is characteristic of Argentina and Paraguay.

I don't want anything to drink.	**No quiero beber nada.** *no keeYE-ro be-BER NA-da*
I haven't had anything to drink yet.	**No he tomado nada de beber aún.** *no e to-MA-do NA-da de be-BER aOON*
Do you want to drink something?	**¿Quieres beber algo?** *keeYE-res be-BER AL-go?*
Do you want to drink some more?	**¿Quieres beber un poco más?** *keeYE-res be-BER oon PO-ko mas?*
Thank you but I still have some.	**Gracias, pero aún tengo algo.** *GRA-seeyas, PE-ro aOON TEN-go AL-go (GRA-theeyas)*

The pronunciation to use in Spain is shown in parentheses.

How about some lunch/dinner?	**¿Te apetece algo de comer/ cenar?** *te a-pe-TE-se AL-go de ko-MER/ se-NAR (the-NAR)*

The pronunciation to use in Spain is shown in parentheses.

| Shall we go to a restaurant? | **¿Vamos a un restaurante?** |
| | *BA-mos a oon res-taw-RAN-te?* |

| Have you ordered? | **¿Has pedido algo?** |
| | *AS pe-DEE-do AL-go?* |

| Do you prefer meat or fish? | **¿Prefieres carne o pescado?** |
| | *pre-feeYE-res KAR-ne o pes-KA-do?* |

You may want to ask this question to a friend before choosing the restaurant, because some specialize in meat and others in seafood. In a regular restaurant with any type of food, this still might be an appropriate question, since the type of wine you select would not be the same.

What type of food would you like to eat?	**¿Qué tipo de comida te apetece comer?**
	ke TEE-po de ko-MEE-da te
	a-pe-TE-se ko-MER?
	(a-pe-TE-the)

Although in Spanish-speaking countries there usually are not as many restaurants featuring ethnic groups' foods as you find in the U.S.A., in many cities you can find a wide variety of restaurants. Immigration in Spain, for example, has increased in recent years, and many emigrants arriving from European countries, Russia, Africa and Latin America make their living by opening restaurants featuring their traditional cuisine. The pronunciation to use in Spain is shown in parentheses.

| Do you want a first course? | **¿Quieres un primer plato?** |
| | *keeYE-res oon pree-MER PLA-to?* |

On the restaurant menu you can find the food classified into appetizers (**entrantes**), first course (pasta or vegetables), second course (fish, meat, seafood), and dessert (fruit, ice cream or cake). The question of the tip is not as strict as in the United States. There is not an "X% minimum" tipping rule, but usually everyone simply decides how much money to give to the waiter/waitress according to the service and the quality of the food.

Will you try this (food)?	**¿Quieres probar este plato?** _keeYE-res pro-BAR ES-te PLA-to?_
Try this.	**Prueba esto.** _PRWE-ba ES-to_
What's it called?	**¿Cómo se llama?** _KO-mo se l-YA-ma?_
I've never tried….	**No lo he probado nunca….** _no lo e pro-BA-do NOON-ka…._
Can you eat meat and fish, or are you vegetarian?	**¿Puedes comer carne y pescado, o eres vegetariana/o?** _PWE-des ko-MER KAR-ne ee pes-KA-do, o E-res be-khe-ta-reeYA-na/o?_

If you're asking a female say **vegetariana**; if you're asking a male, say **vegetariano**.

Yes, I can eat meat and fish.	**Sí, puedo comer carne y pescado.** _SEE, PWE-do ko-MER KAR-ne ee pes-KA-do_
No, I'm vegetarian.	**No, soy vegetariano/a.** _no, soy be-khe-ta-reeYA-no/a_

Say the word with the **o** ending if you're male, and with the **a** ending if you're female.

What's your favorite local food?

¿Cuál es tu comida favorita?
KWAL es too ko-MEE-da
fa-bo-REE-ta?

That looks delicious.

Esto parece sabroso.
ES-to pa-RE-se sa-BRO-so
(pa-RE-the)

The pronunciation to use in Spain is shown in parentheses.

It smells good.

Huele bien.
WE-le beeYEN

Give me more.

Dame más.
DA-me mas

Enough.

Es suficiente.
es soo-fee-seeYEN-te
(soo-fee-theeYEN-te)

The pronunciation to use in Spain is shown in parentheses.

Enough?

¿Tienes suficiente?
teeYE-nes soo-fee-seeYEN-te?
(soo-fee-theeYEN-te)

The pronunciation to use in Spain is shown in parentheses.

Not enough.

No tengo suficiente.
no TEN-go soo-fee-seeYEN-te
(soo-fee-theeYEN-te)

The pronunciation to use in Spain is shown in parentheses.

Do you want some more?

¿Quieres un poco más?
keeYE-res oon PO-ko mas?

In most Spanish-speaking countries it's common to insist on repeatedly offering more food to the guests. Most women think it is polite to ask this question because the guests themselves wouldn't ask for more, even if they wished to. However, what is an extremely polite and nice habit can become in some families an imposition you cannot refuse...and you can find yourself eating more than you wanted to.

Sorry, I can't eat that.

Lo siento, no puedo comer esto.
lo seeYEN-to, no PWE-do ko-MER ES-to

Enjoy it!

¡Que aproveche!
ke a-pro-BE-che!

Do you like it?

¿Te gusta?
te GOOS-ta?

It tastes good.

Está bueno.
es-TA BWE-no

It's an unusual taste.

Tiene un gusto raro.
teeYE-ne oon GOOS-to RA-ro

It's okay.   **Está bien.**
                        es-TA beeYEN

It's not good.   **No está bueno.**
                        no es-TA BWE-no

It doesn't taste good. **No sabe bien.**
                        no SA-be beeYEN

It's awful.   **Está malísimo.**
                        es-TA ma-LEE-see-mo

I'm full.   **Estoy lleno/a.**
                        es-TOY L-YE-no/a

Say the word with the **o** ending if you're male, and with the
a ending if you're female.

This might be the best excuse you can give to someone
who offers you more food, when you cannot eat any more.

Likes and Dislikes
Me Gusta, No Me Gusta **8**

| I like it. | **Me gusta.** |
| | *me GOOS-ta* |

| I like it a lot. | **Me gusta mucho.** |
| | *me GOOS-ta MOO-cho* |

| I love it. | **Me encanta.** |
| | *me en-KAN-ta* |

In Spanish-speaking countries there are different words used to refer to someone's "love" for a thing, as opposed to love for a person. When talking about things, places, food, art and any other phenomenon, there's the verb **encantar** to say how much they adore something. However, when they express their feelings of love for a person, it's with the verb **querer**, as in "**Te quiero.**"

| It's okay/so-so. | **Está bien/regular.** |
| | *es-TA beeYEN/re-goo-LAR* |

| I don't like it very much. | **No me gusta mucho.** |
| | *no me GOOS-ta MOO-cho* |

| I don't like it at all. | **No me gusta nada.** |
| | *no me GOOS-ta NA-da* |

| I hate it. | **Lo odio.** |
| | *lo O-deeyo* |

I really hate it.

Lo detesto.
lo de-TES-to

I want...

Quiero...
keeYE-ro...

I really want...

De verdad quiero...
de ber-DA keeYE-ro...

I don't want...

No quiero...
no keeYE-ro...

I really don't want...

De verdad no quiero...
de ber-DA no keeYE-ro...

I'm busy.

Estoy ocupado/a.
es-TOY o-koo-PA-do/a

Say the word with the **o** ending if you're male, and with the **a** ending if you're female.

I'm happy.

Soy feliz.
soy fe-LEES (fe-LEETH)

The pronunciation to use in Spain is shown in parentheses.

I'm glad to know that...

Me alegra saber que...
me a-LE-gra sa-BER ke...

I'm sad.

Estoy triste.
es-TOY TREES-te

I'm fine.

Estoy bien.
es-TOY beeYEN

For the next sentences, say the word with the **o** ending if you're male, and with the **a** ending if you're female.

I'm mad. / I'm mad at you.	**Estoy enfadado/a. / Estoy enfadado/a contigo.** es-*TOY* en-fa-DA-do/a / es-*TOY* en-fa-DA-do/a kon-TEE-go
I'm ready.	**Estoy listo/a.** es-*TOY* LEES-to/a
I'm tired.	**Estoy cansado/a.** es-*TOY* kan-SA-do/a
I'm surprised / what a surprise.	**Estoy sorprendido/a / ¡Qué sorpresa!** es-*TOY* sor-pren-DEE-do/a / ke sor-PRE-sa!
I'm scared.	**Estoy asustado/a.** es-*TOY* a-soos-TA-do/a
I'm disappointed.	**Estoy desilusionado/a.** es-*TOY* de-see-loo-seeyo-NA-do/a
I was worried.	**Estaba preocupado/a.** es-*TA*-ba pre-o-koo-PA-do/a
I feel sick.	**Me siento mal.** me seeYEN-to mal
What a relief.	**¡Qué alivio!** ke a-LEE-beeo!

I'm tired of it.	**Estoy cansado/a de eso.**
	es-TOY kan-SA-do/a de E-so

Say the word with the **o** ending if you're male, and with the **a** ending if you're female.

I understand.	**Lo entiendo.**
	lo en-teeYEN-do

I think I understand.	**Creo que lo entiendo.**
	KRE-o ke lo en-teeYEN-do

I don't understand.	**No lo entiendo.**
	no lo en-teeYEN-do

Although in English you can say "I know Mr. Brown" and "I know algebra," in Spanish there is a different verb to use for each: **conocer** refers to knowing (being acquainted with) people and places. **Saber** refers to knowing (intellectually) something—it could be events that happened, or subjects in school. The next few expressions reflect this.

I know that person.	**Conozco a esa persona.**
	ko-NOS-ko a E-sa per-SO-na
	(ko-NOTH-ko)

The pronunciation to use in Spain is shown in parentheses, for this and the next two phrases.

Do you know that person?	**¿Conoces a esa persona?**
	ko-NO-ses a E-sa per-SO-na?
	(ko-NO-thes)

Ah, you know that person.	**¡Ah, conoces a esa persona!**
	a, ko-NO-ses a E-sa per-SO-na!
	(ko-NO-thes)

I know.   **Lo sé.**
                         lo SE

I don't know.   **No sé.**
                         no SE

You knew that,   **¿Sabías eso, verdad?**
    didn't you?   *sa-BEEyas E-so, ber-DA?*

Give me time to think   **Dame tiempo para pensarlo.**
    it over.   *DA-me teeYEM-po PA-ra*
                         pen-SAR-lo

I'll think about it.   **Lo pensaré.**
                         lo pen-sa-RE

I'm so confused.   **Estoy muy confundido/a.**
                         es-TOY mooy kon-foon-DEE-do/a

Say the word with the **o** ending if you're male, and with the
a ending if you're female.

I made a mistake.   **Me he equivocado.**
                         me e e-kee-bo-KA-do

I blew it.   **Lo he echado todo a perder.**
                         lo e e-CHA-do TO-do a per-DER

Even though the above two expressions are similar, just as
with the English versions the second is more extreme than
the first as far as the negative effect of one's errors.

Am I right?   **¿Estoy en lo cierto?**
                         es-TOY en lo seeYER-to? (theeYER-to)

The pronunciation to use in Spain is shown in parentheses.

I'm wrong?	**¿Me equivoco?** *me e-kee-BO-ko?*
Too bad / what a pity.	**¡Qué pena!** *ke PE-na!*
I hope so.	**Espero que sí.** *es-PE-ro ke SEE*
Go for it! Good luck!	**¡Pruébalo! ¡Buena suerte!** *prwE-ba-lo! BWE-na SWER-te!*
Calm down.	**Cálmate.** *KAL-ma-te*
Cheer up.	**Anímate.** *a-NEE-ma-te*
Never mind.	**No importa.** *no eem-POR-ta*
Cool.	**Genial / Tranquilo / Guay** *khe-neeYAL / tran-KEE-lo / gwEYE*

You may use **genial** to refer to something great, or just as a way to agree with another person. It can express that you think what's been stated is a good idea. In a different context, "cool" would call for the second option in Spanish, **tranquilo**—it would be the most appropriate reply to a question about your life, like "How's it going." The word **guay** is the slang expression that's most often heard, especially in Spain, and it reflects a certain generation of teenagers, although you can hear it used by older people too. This is the term that encompasses the previous two meanings, but it's very colloquial and not appropriate in a formal situation.

Uncool. **Se enrolla mal.**
se en-RO-l-ya mal

This is also a very colloquial slang expression, with the opposite statement being "**Se enrolla bien.**" It can refer to a person or to an event. There are variants of this expression with similar meanings. For instance you might also hear "**Que buen rollo**" or "**Que mal rollo.**"

Awesome. **Maravilloso. / Fantástico.**
ma-ra-bee-l-YO-so / fan-TAS-tee-ko

Cute. **Mono/a.**
MO-no/a

Although the word literally means "monkey" it has become a metaphor to refer to something or someone you like because it has the peculiar, playful and nice qualities of that species. You can use it for a nice outfit, any kind of object and very often for a person you like…in which case, say the feminine version, "**mona,**" if you're describing a female.

Really cute. **Monísimo.**
mo-NEE-see-mo

Clever/smart. **Inteligente / Brillante.**
in-te-lee-KHEN-te / bree-l-YAN-te

Ugly. **Feo.**
FE-o

Smart ass. **Sabelotodo.**
sa-be-lo-TO-do

This Spanish expression literally translates as "know-it-all." It can be a compliment, and at the same time an insult if you say it with sarcasm. If said with an unfriendly tone of voice, it's as rude as the above English term can be.

Insults and Quarrels
Insultos y Peleas

9

Talking very loudly in public, even screaming, might not mean a fight, but simply arguing about something. At times, though, the tone and volume of the "discussion" can reach an edge suggesting people are about to quarrel or even fight physically. Just as in the United States, in Spanish-speaking countries brawling in public is a behavior that's most often associated with lower classes—not as the norm!

You may or may not encounter a fight while you're traveling in Spain or Latin America, but you never know; so here are some phrases that might come in handy.

During your travels, you'll likely notice that the urban settings you experience are not very different from cities in the U.S., because the media, mainly television, exports the American lifestyle to other countries. In many Latin American countries as well as in Spain, even though the amount of TV violence hasn't yet reached the level found in the U.S., the effects are starting to show in a more violent generation of children and teenagers.

We're making a line.	**Estamos haciendo cola.** *es-TA-mos a-seeYEN-do KO-la* *(a-theeYEN-do)*

The pronunciation to use in Spain is shown in parentheses.

Could you go a bit faster?	**¿Puede ir un poco más rápido?** *PWE-de eer oon PO-ko mas* *RA-pee-do?*

Don't push.   **No empuje.**
             no em-POO-khe

During rush hour in large cities, it is normal to be pushed to make room in the crowded bus or train. Therefore this can also be used just to inform someone that there is simply no more room.

Man, they are slow.   **Son lentos.**
                     son LEN-tos

The service here is   **El servicio aquí es malísimo.**
    so bad.   *el ser-BEE-seeyo a-KEE es*
                          ma-LEE-see-mo (ser-BEE-theeyo)

The pronunciation to use in Spain is shown in parentheses.

Do you want to say   **¿Quieres decir algo?**
    something.   *keeYE-res de-SEER AL-go?*
                         (de-THEER)

The pronunciation to use in Spain is shown in parentheses.

Don't look at me.   **No me mires.**
                    no me MEE-res

Don't stare at me.   **No me mires fijamente.**
                     no me MEE-res fee-kha-MEN-te

The first expression, "**No me mires,**" could be asked when someone wants some privacy, for instance while changing clothes at a public place like the beach. Sometimes it can express some modesty and embarrassment or just a peculiar mood.

The second expression more specifically implies that the other person is deliberately looking at you for too long, indicating for example that he/she would like to start talking, the most obvious way to express interest. The sentence above can be said to cut off that interest.

Pervert!	**¡Pervertido!** *per-ber-TEE-do!*
Vulgar!	**¡Vulgar!** *bool-GAR!*
Take your hands off.	**Quíte sus manos de encima.** *KEE-te soos MA-nos de en-SEE-ma* *(en-THEE-ma)*

This would usually refer to a person who is touching someone inappropriately in a crowd, like in the subway or on the bus. The pronunciation to use in Spain is shown in parentheses.

Don't touch me.	**No me toque.** *no me TO-ke*
This can't be right.	**No es justo.** *no es KHOOS-to*
I think you're tricking me.	**Creo que estás bromeando.** *KRE-o ke es-TAS bro-me-AN-do*

In a previous chapter we saw a similar expression, but with a sarcastic connotation: "**Me estás tomando el pelo**," which can imply anger sometimes. However, any of these idiomatic expressions can be harmless and friendly instead, if said with a nice tone of voice.

This can't be so expensive.	**Esto no puede ser tan caro.** *ES-to no PWE-de ser tan KA-ro*
This is more expensive than what I thought.	**Esto es más caro de lo que pensaba.** *ES-to es mas KA-ro de lo ke pen-SA-ba*

This is different from what I've heard.

Esto es diferente de lo que he escuchado.

ES-to es dee-fe-REN-te de lo ke e es-koo-CHA-do

Don't think I'm stupid.

No creas que soy estúpido/a.

no KRE-as ke soy es-TOO-pee-do/a

Say the word with the **o** ending if you're male, and with the **a** ending if you're female.

Explain to me why.

Explícame porqué.

eks-PLEE-ka-me por-KE

Don't you think you made a mistake?

¿No crees que te has equivocado?

no KRE-es ke te as e-kee-bo-KA-do?

Is this because I'm a foreigner?

¿Es porque soy estranjero?

es POR-ke soy es-tran-KHE-ro?

Is this because I'm an American?

¿Es porque soy Americano/a?

es POR-ke soy a-me-ree-KA-no/a?

Say the word with the **o** ending if you're male, and with the **a** ending if you're female.

I want to talk to the manager.

Quiero hablar con el encargado.

keeYE-ro a-BLAR kon el en-kar-GA-do

I won't come here again.

No voy a volver aquí nunca.

no boy a bol-BER a-KEE noon-KA

I'll tell my friends.

Se lo diré a mis amigos.

se lo dee-RE a mees a-MEE-gos

Hey, tell me your name.

Hola, ¿cómo te llamas?
O-la, KO-mo te L-YA-mas?

You won't get away with this.

No te vas a salir con la tuya.
no te bas a sa-LEER kon la TOO-ya

INSULTS & CURSES
The following are useful expressions to say when someone is angry. Some of them are strong phrases which can trigger an argument and escalate into a fight. Avoid these words unless it is really necessary.

Damn it!

¡Maldita sea!
mal-DEE-ta SE-a!

Shit!

¡Mierda!
meeYER-da!

What a mess.

¡Que lío!
ke LEEyo!

What do you want.

¿Qué quieres?
ke keeYE-res?

What did you say?

¿Qué has dicho?
ke as DEE-cho?

Who do you think you are?	**¿Quién te crees que eres?**
	keeYEN te KRE-es ke E-res?

Why do you talk like that to me?	**¿Por qué me hablas así?**
	por ke me A-blas a-SEE?

Are you stupid or what?	**¿Eres estúpido/a o qué?**
	E-res es-TOO-pee-do/a o ke?

For this phrase and the next two, say the word with the **o** ending if you're speaking to a male, and with the **a** ending if you're speaking to a female.

You're stupid.	**Eres estúpido/a.**
	E-res es-TOO-pee-do/a

You look stupid.	**Pareces estúpido/a.**
	pa-RE-ses es-TOO-pee-do/a
	(pa-RE-thes)

The pronunciation to use in Spain is shown in parentheses.

That's stupid.	**Esto es estúpido.**
	ES-to es es-TOO-pee-do

What you did was stupid.	**Lo que has hecho es estúpido.**
	lo ke as E-cho es es-TOO-pee-do

You're crazy.	**Estás loco/a.**
	es-TAS LO-ko/a

Say the word with the **o** ending if you're speaking to a male, and with the **a** ending if you're speaking to a female.

Stop acting stupid. Don't joke around with me.	**Deja de hacer el estúpido.**
	No bromees conmigo.
	DE-kha de a-SER el es-TOO-pee-do.
	No bro-ME-es con-MEE-go

Don't say stupid things. **No digas cosas estúpidas.**
no DEE-gas KO-sas es-TOO-pee-das

Liar. **Mentiroso/a.**
men-tee-RO-so/a
Say the word with the **o** ending if you're speaking to a male, and with the **a** ending if you're speaking to a female.

That's a lie. **Esto es mentira.**
ES-to es men-TEE-ra

Don't lie. **No digas mentiras.**
no DEE-gas men-TEE-ras

Stop it. **Para ya.**
PA-ra ya
You can also say just "**Para**," but the word **ya**, meaning "already," is very common in this expression.

You shouldn't do that. **No deberías hacer eso.**
no de-be-REEyas a-SER E-so
(a-THER)
The pronunciation to use in Spain is shown in parentheses.

Why do you do **¿Porqué haces cosas como**
things like that. **esa?**
por-KE A-ses KO-sas KO-mo
E-sa?

Leave him/her alone. **Déjalo/la en paz.**
DE-kha-lo/la en pas (path)
The pronunciation to use in Spain is shown in parentheses, here and for the following phrases.

Do as I say.
Haz lo que te digo.
as (ath) lo ke te DEE-go

Not one word more.
Ni una palabra más.
nee OO-na pa-LA-bra MAS

Give it back.
Devuélvemelo/la.
de-BWEL-be-me-lo/la

Leave me alone.
Déjame en paz.
DE-kha-me en pas (path)

Leave us alone.
Déjanos en paz.
DE-kha-nos en pas (path)

Get out of here.
Vete de aquí.
BE-te de a-KEE

Come here.
Ven aquí.
BEN a-KEE

Shut up.
Cállate.
KA-l-ya-te

Don't move.
Estate quieto.
es-TA-te keeYE-to

You asshole.
Eres imbécil.
E-res eem-BEH-seel (eem-BEH-theel)

You are ugly.
Eres feo/a.
E-res FE-o/a

Say the word with the **o** ending if you're speaking to a male, and with the **a** ending if you're speaking to a female.

You pig.

Cerdo.
SER-do (THER-do)

Fag.

Marica.
ma-REE-ka

Don't fuck with me.

No me jodas.
no me KHO-das

Although vulgar, this is a very common slang expression used in many contexts, most of the time when someone cannot take it anymore.

Go to hell.

Vete al infierno.
BE-te al een-feeYER-no

Don't try to be cool.

No te des esos aires.
no te des E-sos aEE-res

The expression is intended for someone who is too arrogant, for who feels they're above the rest, and shows it in their manners.

Let's finish this now.

Vamos a acabar esto ahora.
BA-mos a a-ka-BAR ES-to a-O-ra

Chitchat and Courting
Charlando y Cortejando

10

Are you having a good time?	**¿Te lo pasas bien?** *te lo PA-sas beeYEN?*
You look like you're having a good time.	**Parece que te lo estás pasando bien.** *pa-RE-se ke te lo es-TAS pa-SAN-do beeYEN (pa-RE-the)*

The pronunciation to use in Spain is shown in parentheses.

Yeah, I'm having fun.	**Sí, me estoy divirtiendo.** *SEE, me es-TOY dee-beer-teeYEN-do*
No, not really.	**No, no realmente.** *no, no re-al-MEN-te*
We're having a good time, aren't we?	**¿Nos lo estamos pasando bien, verdad?** *nos lo es-TA-mos pa-SAN-do beeYEN, BER-da?*
Did you two come here by yourselves?	**¿Habéis venido aquí solos/las?** *a-BEees be-NEE-do a-KEE SO-los/las?*
Shall we drink together?	**¿Bebemos algo juntos?** *be-BE-mos AL-go KHOON-tos?*

| Has someone reserved this seat? / Is someone sitting here? | **¿Está reservado este asiento? / ¿Hay alguien sentado aquí?** es-TA re-ser-BA-do ES-te a-seeYEN-to? / eye AL-geeyen sen-TA-do a-KEE? |

Those two questions refer to seats, either in a restaurant or at a performance. You can ask the same thing with a wider meaning like this: "**¿Está reservado?**" With this expression you can refer to any place anywhere, for instance at a concert outdoors without seats, where the public sits on the grass.

Do you want to sit down?	**¿Quieres sentarte?** keeYE-res sen-TAR-te?
May I sit down?	**¿Puedo sentarme?** PWE-do sen-TAR-me?
Let me sit down.	**Déjame sentar.** DE-kha-me sen-TAR.
Shuffle over / make room.	**Déjame sitio.** DE-kha-me SEE-teeyo
Do you like this music?	**¿Te gusta esta música?** te GOOS-ta ES-ta MOO-see-ka?

What music do you like?	**¿Qué tipo de música te gusta?** *ke TEE-po de MOO-see-ka te OOS-ta?*
Whose music do you like?	**¿Qué cantantes te gustan?** *ke kan-TAN-tes te GOOS-tan?*
Do you know this song?	**¿Conoces esta canción?** *ko-NO-ses (ko-NO-thes) ES-ta kan-seeYON (kan-theeYON)*

The pronunciation to use in Spain is shown in parentheses, here and for the next phrases.

I know it.	**La conozco.** *la ko-NOS-ko (ko-NOTH-ko)*
I don't know it.	**No la conozco.** *no la ko-NOS-ko (ko-NOTH-ko)*
Shall we dance?	**¿Bailamos?** *baee-LA-mos?*
I don't feel like dancing yet.	**No tengo ganas de bailar.** *no TEN-go GA-nas de baee-LAR*

You are a good dancer.	**Bailas bien.** *BAEE-las beeYEN*
How do you know of this place?	**¿Cómo conoces este sitio?** *KO-mo ko-NO-ses ES-te SEE-teeyo* *(ko-NO-thes)*
I heard from my friends.	**Por los amigos.** *por los a-MEE-gos*
Where else do you go to dance?	**¿A qué otros sitios vas a bailar?** *a ke O-tros SEE-teeyos bas a baee-LAR*

In most Spanish-speaking countries you can find disco-theques and pubs with live music performances where people can also dance. In summer it's also very common to find outdoor festivals where bands perform and the public dance in the streets. Many times it's to celebrate some holiday like the town's patron saint day, since most of these countries are predominantly Catholic. Usually there are also food and beverages.

How long have you been in Spain?	**¿Cuánto tiempo llevas en España?** *KWAN-to teeYEM-po l-YE-bas en es-PA-nya?*
Let's party!	**¡Vamos a una fiesta! / ¡Demos una fiesta!** *BA-mos a OO-na feeYES-ta! / DE-mos OO-na feeYES-ta!*

The first expression means "let's go to a party," usually at a friend's house, but it can also refer to one of the street cel-ebrations for a local holiday. The second expression means that you are throwing the party for your friends. Usually in Spanish-speaking countries they celebrate birthday parties and other social events with a party, but sometimes people—especially younger people on a weekend—also throw parties just to gather with friends.

Let's get drunk!	**¡Vamos a emborracharnos!**
	BA-mos a em-bo-rra-CHAR-nos!

The sound of the double **r** doesn't exist in English and so it can be difficult to pronounce. It sounds like a strong **r**; let your tongue linger a little bit between the vowels.

What are you drinking?	**¿Qué bebes?**
	ke BE-bes?

Have you been drinking a lot?	**¿Has estado bebiendo mucho?**
	as es-TA-do be-beeYEN-do MOO-cho?

You need to drink more.	**Necesitas beber un poco más.**
	ne-se-SEE-tas be-BER oon PO-ko mas (ne-the-SEE-tas)

This is an invitation to cheerfully encourage someone to drink and make the event enjoyable, however, be careful not to give the impression to someone that you want him/her to be drunk.

The pronunciation to use in Spain is shown in parentheses.

Are you drunk?   **¿Estás borracho/a?**
                  es-TAS bo-RRA-cho/a?

Say the word with the **o** ending if you're speaking to a male,
and with the **a** ending if you're speaking to a female.

Haven't you drunk   **¿Has bebido demasiado?**
    too much?   *AS be-BEE-do de-ma-seeYA-do?*

Maybe you should   **Quizás, deberías parar de**
    stop drinking.   **beber.**
                  kee-SAS de-be-REEyas pa-RAR de
                  be-BER (ke-THAS)

The pronunciation to use in Spain is shown in parentheses.

Are you okay?   **¿Estás bien?**
                  es-TAS beeYEN?

You're nice (kind).   **Eres amable.**
                  E-res a-MA-ble

What time did you   **¿A qué hora has venido aquí?**
    come here?   *a ke O-ra as be-NEE-do a-KEE?*

What time are   **¿A qué hora te vas?**
    you leaving?   *a ke O-ra te bas?*

I haven't decided.   **No lo he decidido.**
                  no lo e de-see-DEE-do
                  (de-thee-DEE-do)

The pronunciation to use in Spain is shown in parentheses.

If I have a good time   **Si me lo paso bien me quedaré.**
    I'll stay.   *see me lo PA-so beeYEN me*
                  ke-da-RE

If this gets boring, I'll go home.	**Si me aburro me iré a casa.** *see me a-BOO-rro me ee-RE a KA-sa*
This is boring!	**¡Esto es aburrido!** *ES-to es a-boo-RREE-do!*
Shall we go somewhere else?	**¿Nos vamos a algún otro sitio?** *nos BA-mos a al-GOON O-tro SEE-teeyo?*
Shall we leave?	**¿Nos vamos?** *nos BA-mos?*
Can my friends come?	**¿Pueden venir mis amigos/as?** *PWE-den be-NEER mees a-MEE-gos/as?*

If the group of friends is mixed male and female, or is only males, you'd say "**amigos**." But if it's only girls, you'd say "**amigas**" instead.

I'd like to stay longer.	**Me gustaría quedarme un poco más.** *me goos-ta-REEYA ke-DAR-me oon PO-ko mas*
What's next?	**¿Qué hacemos después?** *ke a-SE-mos des-PWES?*
Have you decided?	**¿Has decidido ya?** *as de-see-DEE-do ya?* *(de-thee-DEE-do)*

The pronunciation to use in Spain is shown in parentheses, here and for some of the next phrases.

I haven't decided yet.   **No he decidido todavía.**
                           no e de-see-DEE-do to-da-BEEya
                             (de-thee-DEE-do)

It's up to you.   **Depende de tí.**
                           de-PEN-de de TEE

Anything is fine.   **Cualquier cosa está bien.**
                           kwal-keeYER KO-sa es-TA beeYEN

I have a good idea.   **Tengo una buena idea.**
                           TEN-go OO-na BWE-na ee-DE-a

How does that sound?   **¿Qué te parece esto?**
                           ke te pa-RE-se ES-to? (pa-RE-the)

Good idea!   **¡Buena idea!**
                           BWE-na ee-DE-a!

Anywhere is okay.   **Cualquier sitio está bien.**
                           kwal-keeYER SEE-teeyo es-TA
                              beeYEN

I'll take you home.   **Te llevaré a casa.**
                           te l-ye-ba-RE a KA-sa

COURTING / *CORTEJANDO*
The next sentences are some handy phrases for flirting
with someone.

I want to know more   **Quiero conocerte mejor.**
    about you.   *keeYE-ro ko-no-SER-te me-KHOR*
                              (ko-no-THER-te)

The pronunciation to use in Spain is shown in parentheses.

I like talking to you. **Me gusta hablar contigo.**
me GOOS-ta a-BLAR kon-TEE-go

You are so handsome/ **Eres tan guapo/a.**
beautiful. *E-res tan GWA-po/a*

Say the word with the **o** ending if you're speaking to a male, and with the **a** ending if you're speaking to a female.

We think the same **Pensamos de forma parecida,**
way, don't we? / **¿verdad? / Somos muy**
We are so similar. **parecidos.**
pen-SA-mos de FOR-ma
pa-re-SEE-da, ber-DA?
(pa-re-THEE-da) / SO-mos mooy
pa-re-SEE-dos (pa-re-THEE-dos)

The pronunciation to use in Spain is shown in parentheses.

Let's meet again. **Volvamos a encontrarnos.**
bol-BA-mos a en-kon-TRAR-nos

When can I see you **¿Cuándo puedo volver a verte?**
next time? *KWAN-do PWE-do bol-BER a*
BER-te?

Do you want to drink a coffee together tomorrow?	**¿Quieres tomar un café juntos mañana?**
	keeYE-res to-MAR oon ka-FE KHOON-tos ma-NYA-na?
May I call you?	**¿Puedo llamarte?**
	PWE-do l-ya-MAR-te?
May I have your phone number?	**¿Me das tu número de teléfono?**
	me das too NOO-me-ro de te-LE-fo-no?
Do you have something to write with?	**¿Tienes algo para escribir?**
	teeYE-nes AL-go PA-ra es-cree-BEER?
I enjoyed myself.	**He disfrutado.**
	eh dees-froo-TA-do
Take care.	**¡Cuídate!**
	kwEE-da-te!
See you later.	**Hasta luego.**
	AS-ta LWE-go
See you tomorrow.	**Hasta mañana.**
	AS-ta ma-NYA-na
Bye.	**Adiós.**
	a-deeOS

On the Phone
En el Teléfono

11

Hello.

Hola.
O-la

Good morning /
good evening.
Is __ there please?

Buenos días / buenas tardes.
¿Está __ por favor?
BWE-nos DEEyas / BWE-nas
TAR-des. es-TA __ por fa-BOR?

Could you get __
please?

¿Puede llamar a __ por favor?
PWE-de l-ya-MAR a __ por fa-BOR?

Can I speak with __ ?

¿Puedo hablar con __ ?
PWE-do a-BLAR kon __ ?

Hold on please.

Espere (Espera) por favor.
es-PE-re (es-PE-ra) por fa-BOR

In parentheses is the informal (**tú**) form used in colloquial
Spanish, usually when you already know the person. If you
do not recognize the voice, it's more appropriate to say the
formal **usted** form, which is the first one shown.

Hello, this is Robert;
can I please talk to
Maria?

Hola, soy Roberto, ¿puedo
hablar con María por
favor?
O-la, soy Roberto, PWE-do a-BLAR
kon Maria por fa-BOR?

Here she/he is. **Aquí está.**
a-KEE es-TA

I'm sorry, she/ **Lo siento no está aquí.**
he is out. *lo seeYEN-to no es-TA a-KEE*

She/he will be back **Ella/él volverá más tarde.**
later. *E-l-ya/El bol-be-RA mas TAR-de*

Very often in Spanish you don't state the subject in the sentence. So in this case, it would be equally correct to say **"Volverá..."** without the **ella/él** at the beginning.

Can I leave a message? **¿Puedo dejar un mensaje?**
PWE-do de-KHAR oon men-SA-khe?

Can you tell her/him **¿Puede decirle que ha llamado**
that Robert called? **Roberto?**
PWE-de de-SEER-le ke a
l-ya-MA-do Roberto?
(de-THEER-le)

The pronunciation to use in Spain is shown in parentheses.

This is the phone **Este es el teléfono donde**
number where **puede llamarme...**
she/he can call *ES-te es el te-LE-fo-no DON-de*
me back... *PWE-de l-ya-MAR-me...*

I'll tell her/him to **Le diré que vuelva a llamarte.**
call you back. *le dee-RE ke BWEL-ba a l-ya-MAR-te*

CELL PHONES
Teléfonos Móviles (Celulares)

It's very common in Spanish-speaking countries to have a telephone at home and a cell phone too. They're not as frequently found in some areas of the countryside where there's less technology infrastructure, but the cell phone is already in the process of conquering that territory too.

The cell phone is called **móvil** in Spain as the standard term, but in some Spanish-speaking countries due to the English influence they are called **celulares**.

What kind of cell phone did you buy?	**¿Qué tipo de teléfono móvil/ celular has comprado?** *ke TEE-po de te-LE-fo-no MO-beel/ se-loo-LAR as kom-PRA-do? (the-loo-LAR)*

The pronunciation to use in Spain is shown in parentheses, here and for several of the following phrases.

This is really cute.	**Es realmente mono.** *es re-al-MEN-te MO-no*

What's your e-mail address?	**¿Cuál es tu dirección de correo electrónico?** *kwAL es too dee-rek-seeYON de ko-RRE-o e-lek-TRO-nee-ko? (dee-rek-theeYON)*

Even though there is a specific Spanish term, many call it "**e-mail**" instead. This phenomenon happens with many technology words, because they first appeared in the United States.

It's hard to e-mail with this phone.

Es difícil enviar e-mails con este teléfono.

es dee-FEE-seel en-beeYAR ee-mels kon ES-te te-LE-fo-no (dee-FEE-theel)

But I can send instant messages.

Pero puedo enviar mensajes instantáneos.

PE-ro PWE-do en-beeYAR men-SA-khes eens-tan-TA-ne-os

Can you do e-mail in English/Spanish?

¿Puedes enviar e-mails en inglés/español? (correo electrónico)

PWE-des en-beeYAR ee-mels en een-GLES/es-pa-NYOL?

In parentheses is the standard Spanish for "e-mail," since you may encounter someone who does not know the Spanglish term.

Could you teach me?

¿Puedes enseñarme?

PWE-des en-se-NYAR-me?

I'll send you a text message later.

Te enviaré un mensaje luego.

te en-beea-RE oon men-SA-khe LWE-go

How are you doing?

¿Cómo estás?

KO-mo es-TAS?

I've been doing okay.

He estado bien.

e es-TA-do beeYEN

So-so / Not good, not bad.

Así, así / Ni bien, ni mal.

a-SEE, a-SEE / nee beeYEN, nee mal

What were you doing? **¿Qué estabas haciendo?**
ke es-TA-bas a-seeYEN-do?
(a-theeYEN-do)

You're late. **Llegas tarde.**
L-YE-gas TAR-de

I tried to call you. **He tratado de llamarte.**
e tra-TA-do de l-ya-MAR-te

I couldn't find you. **No pude encontrarte.**
no POO-de en-kon-TRAR-te

My (phone) battery **La pila de mi teléfono estaba**
was low. **descargada.**
la PEE-la de mee te-LE-fo-no
es-TA-ba des-kar-GA-da

The line was busy. **La línea de teléfono estaba**
ocupada.
la LEE-ne-a de te-LE-fo-no es-TA-ba
o-koo-PA-da

Who was on the **¿Quién hablaba por teléfono?**
phone? *keeYEN a-BLA-ba por te-LE-fo-no?*

I want to see you. **Quiero verte.**
keeYE-ro BER-te

I want to see you now. **Quiero verte ahora.**
keeYE-ro BER-te a-O-ra

I'll call you again. **Te llamaré luego.**
te l-ya-ma-RE LWE-go

I'll call you after I get there.	**Te llamaré cuando llegue allí.** *te l-ya-ma-RE kwAN-do L-YE-ge a-L-YEE*
What time can I call tomorrow?	**¿A qué hora puedo llamarte mañana?** *a ke O-ra PWE-do l-ya-MAR-te ma-NYA-na?*
I'll call tomorrow at 6 o'clock.	**Te llamaré mañana a las 6 en punto.** *te l-ya-ma-RE ma-NYA-na a las SEees en POON-to*
Please be home.	**Por favor, que estés en casa.** *por fa-BOR, ke es-TES en KA-sa*
Will you be on the Internet tomorrow?	**¿Conectarás el internet mañana?** *ko-nek-ta-RAS el een-ter-NET ma-NYA-na?*

Even though there is a specific term in Spanish for the Internet, which is **red** (**electrónica**), it is very common to say the word in English. In Spanish, many times the word **electrónica** is omitted, because the context lets you know it's the computer and not other types of "net" (which is the literal translation).

Say hello to Clara for me.	**Dile hola a Clara por mí.** *DEE-le O-la a KLA-ra por MEE*

Lovers' Language
La Lengua del Amor **12**

I like you.

Me gustas.
me GOOS-tas

I like you very much.

Me gustas mucho.
me GOOS-tas MOO-cho

I'm attracted to you.

Me atraes.
me a-TRA-es

I feel good being
   with you.

**Me siento bien cuando estoy
contigo.**
*me seeYEN-to beeYEN KWAN-do
   es-TOY kon-TEE-go*

I'm crazy about you.

Me vuelves loco/a.
me BWEL-bes LO-ko/a

Say the word with the **o** ending if you're male, and with the
a ending if you're female.

I love you.

Te quiero.
te keeYE-ro

As we discussed earlier, most often romantic love is
expressed in Spanish with "**te quiero**." This phrase is also
used to express the love you have for your friends or your
family.

I adore you.   **Te adoro.**
                            te a-DO-ro

I'm yours.   **Soy tuyo/a.**
                            soy TOO-I-yo/a
Say the word with the **o** ending if you're male, and with the **a** ending if you're female.

You are mine.   **Eres mío/mía.**
                            E-res MEEyo/MEEya
Say the word with the **o** ending if you're male, and with the **a** ending if you're female.

I want to know all   **Quiero saberlo todo de ti.**
   about you   *keeYE-ro sa-BER-lo TO-do de TEE*

I'll tell you.   **Te lo diré todo.**
                            te lo dee-RE TO-do

You're good-looking/   **Eres guapo/a.**
   beautiful.   *E-res GWA-po/a*
Say the word with the **o** ending if you're speaking to a male, and with the **a** ending if you're speaking to a female.

More often men give this type of compliment to women. There are occasions when a woman might say these words to a male, but mostly it would be when talking to a child or a baby. It's not very common to hear it said to an adult male, unless there is a romantic relationship between the two of them.

You're attractive /   **Eres atractiva/o. / Eres sexy.**
   You're sexy.   *E-res a-trac-TEE-bo/a /*
                            E-res SEK-see
Say the word with the **o** ending if you're speaking to a male, and with the **a** ending if you're speaking to a female.

Look at me.
Mírame.
MEE-ra-me

You have beautiful eyes.
Tienes los ojos bonitos.
teeYE-nes los O-khos bo-NEE-tos

I want to be close to you.
Quiero estar cerca de ti.
keeYE-ro es-TAR SER-ka de tee
(THER-ka)

The pronunciation to use in Spain is shown in parentheses.

May I kiss you?
¿Puedo besarte?
PWE-do be-SAR-te?

Kiss me.
Bésame.
BE-sa-me

I want to hold you tight.
Quiero abrazarte.
keeYE-ro a-bra-SAR-te
(a-bra-THAR-te)

The pronunciation to use in Spain is shown in parentheses.

I want to come and visit you in America.
Quiero ir a visitarte a América.
keeYE-ro eer a bee-see-TAR-te a
a-ME-ree-ka

I want to come back to Spain/Costa Rica for you.
Quiero volver a España/Costa Rica a visitarte.
keeYE-ro bol-BER a es-PA-nya/
KOS-ta REE-ka a bee-see-TAR-te

I want to stay with you forever.
Quiero estar contigo para siempre.
keeYE-ro es-TAR kon-TEE-go PA-ra
seeYEM-pre

Shall we think about
getting married?

**¿Crees que deberíamos
casarnos?**
*KRE-es ke de-be-reeYA-mos
ka-SAR-nos?*

Will you marry me?

¿Quieres casarte conmigo?
keeYE-res ka-SAR-te kon-MEE-go?

This marriage proposal is very direct and secure, there is no
doubt about it, compared to the previous one which shows
some uncertainty. In the previous expression, though, the
person may simply be unsure whether this is the right time
to do it—not necessarily unsure about getting married!

I'm not ready to talk
about marriage
yet.

**No estoy listo/a para hablar
de matrimonio.**
*no es-TOY LEES-to/a PA-ra a-BLAR
de ma-tree-MO-neeyo*

Say the word with the **o** ending if you're male, and with the
a ending if you're female.

I don't want to get
married yet.

No quiero casarme todavía.
*no keeYE-ro ka-SAR-me
to-da-BEEya*

I don't want to think
about marriage yet.

**No quiero pensar en el
matrimonio todavía.**
*no keeYE-ro pen-SAR en el
ma-tree-MO-neeyo to-da-BEEya*

I love you but I can't marry you.	**Te quiero pero no puedo casarme contigo.** *te keeYE-ro PE-ro no PWE-do ka-SAR-me kon-TEE-go*
It's not time for me to get serious.	**No es el momento adecuado para tener una relación seria.** *no es el mo-MEN-to a-de-KWA-do PA-ra te-NER OO-na re-la-seeYON (re-la-theeYON) SE-reeya*

The pronunciation to use in Spain is shown in parentheses.

Don't get me wrong.	**No te lo tomes a mal.** *no te lo TO-mes a mal*
I'm not good for you.	**No soy la persona adecuada para ti.** *no soy la per-SO-na a-de-KWA-da PA-ra tee*
Forget about me.	**Olvídame.** *ol-BEE-da-me*
I need time to myself.	**Necesito tiempo para mí mismo.** *ne-se-SEE-to teeYEM-po PA-ra mee MEES-mo (ne-the-SEE-to)*

The pronunciation to use in Spain is shown in parentheses.

I'll be in touch.	**Te llamaré.** *te l-ya-ma-RE*

Making Love
Haciendo el Amor

13

In this chapter you can find some necessary expressions for engaging in a more intimate relationship with someone. Although there is a stereotype of the Latin lover, very passionate, flirtatious and seductive, it is a component of this seduction to act gallantly. There are ways to stop someone if they're doing something the other person does not like, so be tactful and aware of nonverbal cues. Asking certain intimate questions in Spanish-speaking countries can make a person feel uncomfortable. However, some words you might say in your own language but that you don't know how to say in Spanish can be replaced by body language.

Although the mentality in Spain and Latin American countries as far as sexual relationships has evolved, it is still not as open as it is in the United States, especially among teenagers. Openness in conversing about sex with someone you do not know very well could be taken as a vulgar and impolite approach in Spanish-speaking countries.

Be careful about these phrases—do not ask questions that could make your partner feel embarrassed or uncomfortable. Explore the territory before stepping in, because some questions can be interpreted as abusive and invasive. Be as respectful as you can in this matter, and remember that often women in those countries have been raised in a more conservative manner. Sometimes gestures can be the most eloquent language, because some girls still expect men to behave like gentlemen.

Can I walk you home?   **¿Puedo acompañarte a casa?**
                        PWE-do a-kom-pa-NYAR-te a KA-sa?

It's a beautiful night,   **¿Es una noche muy bonita,**
    isn't it?   **verdad?**
                        es OO-na NO-che mooy bo-NEE-ta,
                        ber-DA?

Do you want to go   **¿Quieres salir a tomar el aire?**
    out for some   *keeYE-res sa-LEER a to-MAR el*
    fresh air?   *AEE-re?*

Can we hold hands?   **¿Podemos cogernos de la**
                            mano?
                        po-DE-mos ko-KHER-nos de la
                        MA-no?

Take my hand.   **Coge mi mano.**
                        KO-khe mee MA-no

Let me put my arm   **Déjame poner mi brazo en tus**
    around your   **hombros.**
    shoulders.   *DE-kha-me po-NER mee BRA-so*
                        en toos OM-bros (BRA-tho)

The pronunciation to use in Spain is shown in parentheses.

Do you want to   **¿Quieres reclinarte en mí?**
    lean on me?   *keeYE-res re-klee-NAR-te en mee?*

It's a starry night.   **Hace una noche muy**
                            estrellada.
                        A-se OO-na NO-che mooy
                        es-tre-L-YA-da

Would you like to go to the seashore tonight?	**¿Quieres ir a la orilla del mar esta noche?** *keeYE-res eer a la o-REE-I-ya del mar ES-ta NO-che?*
It's too early (to go to sleep).	**Es muy temprano (para ir a dormir).** *es mooy tem-PRA-no (PA-ra eer a dor-MEER)*

The pronunciation to use in Spain is shown in parentheses, here and for several of the below phrases.

Take me tonight.	**Tómame en tus brazos.** *TO-ma-me en toos BRA-sos (BRA-thos)*
	Hagamos el amor esta noche. *a-GA-mos el a-MOR ES-ta NO-che*
	Hazme tuya/o esta noche. *AS-me TOO-ya/o ES-ta NO-che (ATH-me)*

Say the third phrase above with the **o** ending if you're male, and with the **a** ending if you're female.

Although the previous sentence in English implies the couple is about to make love, in Spanish you often find that people are not so direct in this aspect and would rather spend some time in "foreplay," verbal and otherwise. The first sentence is most appropriate, unless the couple know each other very well. Since vacations are usually brief this may not be the case, so keep in mind that you can scare a girl if you propose sexual relations this directly.

Shall we go to a hotel?   **¿Vamos a un hotel?**
BA-mos a oon o-TEL?

This question could be necessary if you're staying in a shared room, for instance, or at a camping site. But if you're staying in your own hotel room it would be more appropriate to ask "**¿Vamos a mi hotel?**" (Shall we go to my hotel?). Usually the invitation implies it's to have some drinks and talk...although if you're a woman and someone asks you this question and you accept, a man may assume you are willing to have sex. If you are not interested you shouldn't accept this type of invitation or you will be very embarrassed.

Although the below questions are not directly related to making love to someone, they are an important part of the ritual in Spanish-speaking countries, where it's rare to jump directly into sex with someone you do not know very well. These phrases are also a good way to make someone feel comfortable and lose some inhibition. This sort of conversational foreplay is many times part of the necessary preliminaries of lovemaking; keep in mind that in Spanish-speaking cultures some people are a little old-fashioned in this respect, and even though attitudes toward sex have changed in recent times, it is still uncommon to disregard the fabled Latin/Spanish lovemaking that relies on creating ambience and romantic buildup.

Do you want to listen to music?	**¿Quieres escuchar música?** *keeYE-res es-koo-CHAR MOO-see-ka?*
Do you want something to drink?	**¿Quieres beber algo?** *keeYE-res be-BER AL-go?*
What would you like to drink?	**¿Qué quieres beber?** *ke keeYE-res be-BER?*
What do you have to drink?	**¿Qué tienes para beber?** *ke teeYE-nes PA-ra be-BER?*
I have beer, juice and wine.	**Tengo cerveza, jugo de frutas y vino.** *TEN-go ser-BE-sa, KHOO-go de FROO-tas y BEE-no (ther-BE-tha)*
I'd have a beer/ juice/wine.	**Tomaré una cerveza / jugo de frutas / vino.** *to-ma-RE OO-na ser-BE-sa / KHOO-go de FROO-tas / BEE-no (ther-BE-tha)*
Are you hungry?	**¿Tienes hambre?** *teeYE-nes AM-bre?*
Yes, what do you have to eat?	**Sí, ¿Qué tienes para comer?** *SEE, ke teeYE-nes PA-ra ko-MER?*

I have some snacks: almonds, peanuts…	**Tengo algunos aperitivos: almendras, cacahuetes …** *TEN-go al-GOO-nos a-pe-ree-TEE-bos: al-MEN-dras, ka-ka-WE-tes…*
Come closer to me.	**Acércate más.** *a-SER-ka-te mas (a-THER-ka-te)*

Remember, the pronunciation to use in Spain is shown in parentheses, here and for several of the following phrases.

I want to caress you.	**Quiero acariciarte.** *keeYE-ro a-ka-ree-seeYAR-te.* *(a-ka-ree-theeYAR-te)*
I'm so glad I waited.	**Me alegro de haber esperado.** *me a-LE-gro de a-BER es-pe-RA-do*
Your hair smells good.	**Tu pelo huele bien.** *too PE-lo WE-le beeYEN*
What perfume/ cologne are you wearing?	**¿Qué perfume/colonia llevas?** *ke per-FOO-me/ko-LO-neeya L-YE-bas?*
I like your eyes.	**Me gustan tus ojos.** *me GOOS-tan toos O-khos*
What color underwear are you wearing?	**¿De qué color es tu ropa interior?** *de ke ko-LOR es too RO-pa een-te-reeYOR?*
I like your underwear.	**Me gusta tu ropa interior.** *me GOOS-ta too RO-pa een-te-reeYOR*

That tickles.

Me haces cosquillas.
me A-ses kos-KEE-l-yas (A-thes)

You have beautiful
skin.

Tienes la piel muy bonita.
*teeYE-nes la peeYEL mooy
bo-NEE-ta*

I found your
birthmark.

**He encontrado tu marca de
nacimiento.**
*e en-kon-TRA-do too MAR-ka de
na-see-meeYEN-to
(na-thee-meeYEN-to)*

Can I kiss you?

¿Puedo besarte?
PWE-do be-SAR-te?

Embrace me!

¡Abrázame!
a-BRA-sa-me! (a-BRA-tha-me)

Hold me in your arms!

¡Tómame en tus brazos!
*TO-ma-me en toos BRA-sos!
(BRA-thos)*

I like your lips/mouth.

Me gustan tus labios/boca.
*me GOOS-tan toos LA-beeyos/
BO-ka*

I'm getting excited.	**Me estoy emocionando/a / excitando/a.** *me es-TOY e-mo-seeYO-nan-do/a /* *eks-see-TAN-do/a* *(e-mo-theeYO-nan-do/a /* *eks-thee-TAN-do/a)*

This expression can have two meanings: the first word option above is about feeling emotional, and the second one is about being turned on. Choose the right one according to the situation.

Do you have a condom?	**¿Tienes un condón?** *teeYE-nes oon kon-DON?*
Will you use a condom?	**¿Usarás un condón?** *oo-sa-RAS oon kon-DON?*
I'll use a condom.	**Usaré un condón.** *oo-sa-RE oon kon-DON*
Are you on the Pill?	**¿Tomas la píldora (anticonceptiva)?** *TO-mas la PEEL-do-ra* *(an-tee-kon-sep-TEE-ba)* *(an-tee-kon-thep-TEE-ba)*

When was your
first experience?

**¿Cuándo tuviste tu primera
experiencia?**
*KWAN-do too-BEES-te too pree-
ME-ra eks-pe-reeYEN-seeya?
(eks-pe-reeYEN-theeya)*

Where was your
first experience?

**¿Dónde tuviste tu primera
experiencia?**
*DON-de too-BEES-te too pree-
ME-ra eks-pe-reeYEN-seeya?
(eks-pe-reeYEN-theeya)*

Who was your first?

¿Quién fue el primero/a?
keeYEN fwe el pree-ME-ro/a?

I did it at… / with…

Lo hice en… / con…
lo EE-se en… (EE-the) / kon…

I'm not going to
tell you.

No te lo voy a decir.
no te lo boy a de-SEER (de-THEER)

How was your
first experience?

**¿Cómo fue tu primera
experiencia?**
*KO-mo fwe too pree-ME-ra
eks-pe-reeYEN-seeya?
(eks-pe-reeYEN-theeya)*

Do you want to take
a shower/bath?

**¿Quieres tomar una ducha/
baño?**
*keeYE-res to-MAR OO-na DOO-cha/
BA-nyo?*

Do you like to do it in the shower/bath?	**¿Te gusta hacerlo en la ducha/ bañera?** *te GOOS-ta a-SER-lo en la DOO-cha/ ba-NYE-ra?*
Do you like to do it in the morning?	**¿Te gusta hacerlo por la mañana?** *te GOOS-ta a-SER-lo por la ma-NYA-na? (a-THER-lo)*
Do you masturbate?	**¿Te masturbas?** *te mas-TOOR-bas?*
Just joking.	**Era broma.** *E-ra BRO-ma*
buttocks	**nalgas** *NAL-gas*
waist	**cintura** *seen-TOO-ra (theen-TOO-ra)*
hips	**caderas** *ka-DE-ras*
belly button	**ombligo** *om-BLEE-go*
breast(s)	**pecho(s) / teta(s)** *PE-cho(s) / TE-ta(s)*

The first is the colloquial word in standard Spanish. The second term is the very informal word; it is not vulgar, but should be used in the right context, for instance when you already know someone well enough to speak in that sort of casual register.

nipple(s) **pezón(es)**
pe-SON(es) (pe-THON(es))

earlobe **lóbulo de tu oreja**
LO-boo-lo de too o-RE-kha

nape of the neck **la nuca**
la NOO-ka

down there **ahí abajo**
a-EE a-BA-kho

The **h** is silent in Spanish, no matter in which position of the word you find it.

bush **espeso**
es-PE-so

cunt **coño**
KO-nyo

cock **agudo**
a-GOO-do

hard-on **duro**
DOO-ro

to come **llegar**
l-ye-GAR

balls **pelotas / cojones**
pe-LO-tas / ko-KHO-nes

The first word is slang, but very often used in colloquial Spanish. The second term is the literal standard translation.

Remember, the pronunciation to use in Spain is shown in parentheses, here and for several of the following phrases.

Caress my nipples/ breast.	**Acaricia mis pezones/pechos.** *a-ka-REE-theeya mees pe-SO-nes (pe-THO-nes)/PE-chos*
Show me what turns you on / stimulates you.	**Dime lo que te excita.** *DEE-me lo ke te eks-SEE-ta*
I like to try different styles.	**Me gusta probar diferentes estilos.** *me GOOS-ta pro-BAR dee-fe-REN-tes es-TEE-los*
Let's change the position.	**Vamos a cambiar de posición** *BA-mos a kam-beeYAR de po-see-seeYON (po-see-theeYON)*
I'm tired of that one.	**Estoy cansado/a de esta.** *es-TOY kan-SA-do/a de ES-ta*

Say the word with the **o** ending if you're male, and with the **a** ending if you're female.

That's original.	**Esto es original.** *ES-to es o-ree-khee-NAL*
That sounds exciting.	**Esto suena excitante.** *ES-to SWE-na ek-see-TAN-te (ek-thee-TAN-te)*

Do you want to do it again?	**¿Quieres que volvamos a hacerlo?** *keeYE-res ke bol-BA-mos a a-SER-lo?* *(a-THER-lo)*
missionary position / girl bottom, boy top	**la posición del misionario** *la po-see-seeYON del mee-seeyo-NA-reeyo (po-see-theeYON)*
boy bottom, girl top	**el hombre abajo, la mujer encima** *el OM-bre a-BA-kho la moo-KHER en-SEE-ma (en-THEE-ma)*
I forgot to use a condom.	**Me he olvidado de usar condón.** *me e ol-bee-DA-do de oo-SAR kon-DON*
I forgot to bring a condom.	**Me he olvidado de traer un condón.** *me e ol-bee-DA-do de tra-ER oon kon-DON*
Did it hurt?	**¿Te he hecho daño?** *te e E-cho DA-nyo?*
It did!	**¡Me has hecho daño!** *me as E-cho DA-nyo!*
No, it didn't.	**No, no me has hecho daño.** *no, no me as E-cho DA-nyo*

In your country, do couples have sex in cars?	**En tu país ¿las parejas hacen el amor en el coche?** *en too paEES, las pa-RE-khas A-sen el a-MOR en el KO-che? (A-then)*
Yes, sometimes.	**Sí, a veces.** *SEE, a BE-ses (BE-thes)*
No. There aren't any good places.	**No, no hay buenos sitios.** *no, no eye BWE-nos SEE-teeyos*
Where do they go?	**¿Adónde van?** *a-DON-de ban?*
Let's find a good place.	**Encontremos un buen sitio.** *en-kon-TRE-mos oon bwen SEE-teeyo*
How do you know of this place?	**¿Cómo has sabido de este sitio?** *KO-mo as sa-BEE-do de ES-te SEE-teeyo?*
People can see us here.	**La gente puede vernos aquí.** *la KHEN-te PWE-de BER-nos a-KEE*
Let's find another place.	**Vamos a encontrar otro sitio.** *BA-mos a en-kon-TRAR O-tro SEE-teeyo*
Let's get in the back seat.	**Vamos al asiento de atrás.** *BA-mos al a-seeYEN-to de a-TRAS*

Let's recline the front seats.

Reclinemos los asientos delanteros.
re-klee-NE-mos los a-seeYEN-tos de-lan-TE-ros

Let's use the blanket.

Usemos la manta.
OO-SE-mos la MAN-ta

The blanket's dirty.

La manta está sucia.
la MAN-ta es-TA SOO-seeya
(SOO-theeya)

Take your shoes off.

Sácate los zapatos.
SA-ka-te los sa-PA-tos (tha-PA-tos)

Relax.

Relájate.
re-LA-kha-te

Enjoy yourself.

Disfruta. / Goza.
dees-FROO-ta / GO-sa (GO-tha)

The first term can refer to any situation, whereas the second refers to sexual intercourse.

Take your ... off.

Sácate tu ... / Quítate tu ...
SA-ka-te too ... / KEE-ta-te too ...

Are you cold?

¿Tienes frío?
teeYE-nes FREEyo?

I'm cold.

Tengo frío.
TEN-go FREEyo

Make me warm.

Hazme entrar en calor.
AS-me en-TRAR en ka-LOR
(ATH-me)

I like you very much.	**Me gustas mucho.** *me GOOS-tas MOO-cho*
You are very… interesting.	**Eres muy…interesante.** *E-res mooy…een-te-re-SAN-te*

Doesn't that feel
    better?
	¿Te hace sentir mejor?
	te A-se sen-TEER me-KHOR?
	    (A-the)

Do it like this.	**Hazlo así.** *AS-lo a-SEE (ATH-lo)*
That's right.	**Así está bien.** *a-SEE es-TA beeYEN*
I made love.	**He hecho el amor.** *e E-cho el a-MOR*
I scored (with her).	**Me la he tirado.** *me la e tee-RA-do*

This is an idiomatic expression, very colloquial, but commonly used. Most frequently a man will say it, not a woman. However, if a female wants to confess the act she would simply say the pronoun **lo** in this sentence instead.

I had sex with her/him.	**Me he acostado con ella/él.** *me e a-kos-TA-do kon E-l-ya/el*
I didn't sleep with her/him.	**No me he acostado con ella/él.** *no me e a-kos-TA-do kon E-l-ya/el*

Love that Comes, Love that Goes
Amor que Viene, Amor que Va

I'm sorry it didn't work out.	**Siento que no funcione entre nosotros.** *seeYEN-to ke no foon-seeYO-ne EN-tre no-SO-tros*
It's over.	**Se ha acabado todo.** *se a a-ka-BA-do TO-do*
Don't be persistent.	**No insistas.** *no een-SEES-tas*
I don't want to see you anymore.	**No quiero volver a verte más.** *no keeYE-ro bol-BER a BER-te más*
Do you have another boyfriend/girlfriend?	**¿Tienes otro novio/novia?** *teeYE-nes O-tro NO-beeyo/ NO-beeya?*
I have another boyfriend/ girlfriend.	**Tengo otro novio/novia.** *TEN-go O-tro NO-beeyo/NO-beeya*
I can't see you anymore.	**No puedo volver a verte.** *no PWE-do bol-BER a BER-te*

I won't call you anymore.	**No te llamaré más.** *no te l-ya-ma-RE mas*
I'm not interested in you anymore.	**Ya no estoy interesado en ti.** *ya no es-TOY een-te-re-SA-do en tee*

Being with you is not fun.	**Estar contigo no es divertido.** *es-TAR kon-TEE-go no es dee-ber-TEE-do*
Stop bothering me.	**Deja de molestarme.** *DE-kha de mo-les-TAR-me*
You don't love me anymore, do you?	**¿Ya no me quieres, verdad?** *ya no me keeYE-res, ber-DA?*
I don't like you anymore.	**Ya no me gustas.** *ya no me GOOS-tas*
I'm sorry, I haven't been a good boyfriend/ girlfriend.	**Lo siento, no he sido un buen novio/novia para ti.** *lo seeYEN-to, no e SEE-do oon bwen NO-beeyo/NO-beeya PA-ra tee*

It's my fault.   **Es culpa mía.**
es KOOL-pa MEEya

Please understand   **Por favor, comprende mis**
my feelings.   **sentimientos.**
por fa-BOR, kom-PREN-de mees
sen-tee-meeYEN-tos

I'll never forget you.   **No te olvidaré nunca.**
no te ol-bee-da-RE NOON-ka

I'm so happy to have   **Soy muy feliz de haberte**
known you.   **conocido.**
soy mooy fe-LEES de a-BER-te
ko-no-SEE-do (fe-LEETH)...
(ko-no-THEE-do)

The pronunciation to use in Spain is shown in parentheses,
here and for several of the following phrases.

Remember me   **Acuérdate de mí alguna vez.**
sometimes.   a-kwER-da-te de mee al-GOO-na
bes (beth)

Can we still be friends?   **¿Podemos continuar siendo amigos?**
po-DE-mos kon-tee-NWAR seeYEN-do a-MEE-gos?

Let's start again.   **Empecemos otra vez.**
em-pe-SE-mos O-tra bes.
(em-pe-THE-mos)…(beth)

I'll always love you.   **Siempre te querré.**
seeYEM-pre te ke-RRE

Can't we start again?   **¿Podemos empezar otra vez?**
po-DE-mos em-pe-SAR O-tra bes?
(em-pe-THAR)…(beth)

I'm serious about you.   **Voy en serio contigo.**
boy en SE-reeyo kon-TEE-go

I can't live without you.   **No puedo vivir sin tí.**
no PWE-do bee-BEER seen tee

I'm so happy to have known you.   **Soy tan feliz de haberte conocido.**
soy tan fe-LEES de a-BER-te ko-no-SEE-do (fe-LEETH)…
(ko-no-THEE-do)

I'll miss you.   **Te echaré de menos.**
te e-cha-RE de ME-nos

I'll always think of you.   **Siempre pensaré en tí.**
seeYEM-pre pen-sa-RE en tee

I'll write you letters/e-mails.

Te escribiré cartas/e-mails.
te es-cree-bee-RE KAR-tas/ee-MELS

Will you write me letters?

¿Me escribirás?
me es-kree-bee-RAS?

Will you send me e-mails?

¿Me escribirás e-mails?
me es-cree-bee-RAS ee-MELS?

I'll call you when I return.

Te llamaré cuando vuelva.
te l-ya-ma-RE KWAN-do BWEL-ba

I have to go because of my job.

Tengo que irme por mi trabajo.
TEN-go ke EER-me por mee tra-BA-kho

Please wait for my return.

Por favor espera mi regreso.
por fa-BOR es-PE-ra mee re-GRE-so

Don't cry.

No llores.
no L-YO-res

Wipe your tears.

Sécate las lágrimas.
SE-ka-te las LA-gree-mas

Take care of yourself.

Cuídate.
KWEE-da-te

I'll be back soon.

Volveré pronto.
bol-be-RE PRON-to